教育部基础学科拔尖学生培养计划 2.0 项目(20212060)
山东省高等教育本科教学改革研究重点项目(Z2022113)
拔尖创新人才英语系列教材

中华文化传播(上)

Introducing Traditional Chinese Culture

丛书主编　周小兰
主　　编　李　红　周小兰
副 主 编　左　宁　孙路平　陈登峰
编　　者　董艳灵　赵　鹏　薛冠琳　李钧秀

山东大学出版社
SHANDONG UNIVERSITY PRESS
·济南·

图书在版编目(CIP)数据

中华文化传播. 上:汉文、英文 / 李红,周小兰主编. —济南:山东大学出版社,2023.1
ISBN 978-7-5607-7575-3

Ⅰ. ①中… Ⅱ. ①李… ②周… Ⅲ. ①中华文化—文化传播—汉、英 Ⅳ. ①G125

中国版本图书馆 CIP 数据核字(2022)第 147364 号

责任编辑 孙艳凤
封面设计 牛 钧

中华文化传播(上)
ZHONGHUA WENHUA CHUANBO(SHANG)

出版发行 山东大学出版社
社　　址 山东省济南市山大南路 20 号
邮政编码 250100
发行热线 (0531)88363008
经　　销 新华书店
印　　刷 济南乾丰云印刷科技有限公司
规　　格 787 毫米×1092 毫米 1/16
　　　　 12.5 印张 280 千字
版　　次 2023 年 1 月第 1 版
印　　次 2023 年 1 月第 1 次印刷
定　　价 48.00 元

Contents

Unit 1 Traditional Festivals

Part A The Chinese New Year

A1. Introduction

The Lunar New Year: Rituals and Legends

For Chinese, in China and in ethnic communities around the world, the lunar new year is the most important and most festive holiday of the year. Through centuries of China's agrarian tradition, this was the one period when farmers could rest from their work in the fields. Family members from near and far would travel to be with loved ones in time to usher out the old year and welcome in the new. All over China, during the Spring Festival, passenger trains, buses, and river boats are packed with holiday travelers; shops do a flurry of business selling gifts, new clothes, and festive foods; kitchens are bustling with preparations for elaborate feasts; and streets are filled with the sounds of firecrackers and seasonal greetings.

Preparations for the New Year

Preparations for New Year festivities begin well in advance of the actual date of the holiday. As the old year draws to a close, there is a tendency to want to tie up loose ends, to put things in order in anticipation of beginning the new year with a fresh start and a clean slate.

Domestically there is a traditional cleansing. In decades past, the most thorough "spring cleaning" of the year was initiated as a ritualistic sweeping away of all the evil spirits feared to be lurking in dark corners behind heavy and rarely moved pieces of furniture. In much of China, peasants waited until the 23rd (in the south of China) or the 24th (in the north) to pick up the broom and dust pan.

Shopping is another major activity of the holiday season. Flowers to brighten the house are a popular item in the markets at this time of year. Wax plum, fragrant white jonquils or narcissus and small peach trees are among the seasonal favorites. So-called New Year prints were another item which for centuries were associated with the New Year Festival in much of China. Also sold in large quantity, for those who couldn't write their own, were couplets and single auspicious characters handwritten on bright red paper.

New Year's Eve

By New Year's Eve, family members, some of whom may have traveled long distances to return home, gather for a reunion.

Traditionally, on this last night of the year, the male head of the household led the family in making offerings to various gods of the house and to the ancestors. Younger family members would *ketou* to members of each generation above them, in order, beginning with the eldest.

With the rites of ancestor "worship" complete, the family sat down to prepare their biggest meal of the year. Often, a place was set for those members who could not return home. In a tradition still observed today, the dishes served on this evening are chosen for the significance of their names or appearances. For Northerners, one custom still widely observed is the consumption of *jiaozi*, or meat-filled dumplings, at midnight.

Sometime before the rooster crowed, the head of the traditional Chinese family would unseal the front door, amidst explosions of long whips of firecrackers, throwing it open to let in the strong and healthy influences of the fresh year. In years past, few people went to bed on New Year's Eve. A modern Chinese family might stay up late taking advantage of the many special holiday programs broadcast on radio and television. Their ancestors probably passed the first hours of the dawning new year playing games, drinking wine, singing, joking, and telling stories — purposefully making it a night of merriment, which they hoped would set a pattern for the entire year to come.

New Year Festivities

The custom of some families was to wait until the first day of the year to ceremoniously open the main gate or door. Children in some households awoke the morning of New Year's Day to find *hongbao* (red envelopes) under their pillows.

On New Year's Day and for the next several days, people still follow the custom of exchanging visits — with close relatives first, then with distant relatives and friends. Traditionally, the first day was usually devoted to paternal family relatives. In some areas the second day was the day wives went home to visit their natal families, taking children to see their maternal grandparents.

When relatives and friends visit, it is important to serve "lucky" food. One such dish is a platter of dates, peanuts, dried longans, and lotus seeds. In the common Chinese linguistic practice of combining component parts of compound words to form a composite term, the dish is referred to as *zaoshengguizi*, or *lianshengguizi*, which respectively sound like phrases meaning "to soon realize the birth of noble sons," and "the continuous birth of noble sons."

In the days after the new year, it is common to make pilgrimages to temples. Theater groups and acrobatic troupes perform in the streets at marketplaces, on temple grounds, or at large public stadiums. Dragon dances, lion dances, stilt-walking performances, and folk pageantry are still particularly popular. In contemporary China, many parents take their children on outings to the park, the zoo, or the movies.

The Lantern Festival

The 15th day of the first lunar month is known as the "Lantern Festival." The Lantern Festival signals the end of the New Year Festival period.

Originally, lanterns were said to have been used on this night to help see the gods by torch light. Each family would construct an claboratc paper lantern for this purpose. Now in many parts of China there is great emphasis on the craftsmanship used in making exquisite lanterns in a variety of shapes and styles, which are then often shown at public exhibitions.

The Lantern Festival is another occasion for inviting guests and holding feasts, though on a smaller scale than the New Year's Eve celebrations. Children can be seen parading around outside carrying colorful paper lanterns. A common festival pastime is to guess answers to riddles written on slips of paper and attached to a lantern.

By now the new year is already half way into the first month, and virtually everything has returned to normal routine. Businesses have reopened, schools are back in session, and farmers have returned to their labor. The very existence of the society depends on the cyclical pattern of agricultural production, and by extension, the cyclical pattern of the seasons. The calendar says it is time for the first rains of the year, and fields must be readied. A new cycle is well under way.

(Adapted from *columbia.edu*)

A2. Words and Expressions

Vocabulary

1. folklore /ˈfəʊklɔː(r) / *n*. 民间传说,民俗
2. mythical / ˈmɪθɪkl / *adj*. 神话的;想象的,虚构的
3. harass / həˈræs / *v*. 骚扰
4. subdue / səbˈdjuː / *v*. 镇压,制服
5. deity /ˈdeɪəti / *n*. 神,神性
6. immortal / ɪˈmɔːtl / *n*. 不死的;流芳百世的

春节的起源	**Origin of the Spring Festival**
故事和传说	tales and legends
民间故事	folk tale
中国民间传说	Chinese folklore
神话故事	mythology
各种各样的说法	various theories
传说中叫"年"的神兽	a mythical beast called the "Nian"
捕食人类	prey on human beings
骚扰村民和他们的牲畜	harass villagers and their domestic animals
来帮助某人	come to one's rescue
镇压,制服	subdue
贴红纸放爆竹	put red papers up and set off firecrackers
神,神灵	deity
吓得躲到了密林里	be scared off into the forests
吓走神兽"年"	frighten away the "Nian"
穿红衣服	wear red clothes
挂红灯笼	hang red lanterns
门窗上装饰红色	put up red paper decorations on windows and doors
幸福祥和地生活	enjoy their life in peace and happiness

Vocabulary

1. imbue /ɪmˈbjuː / *v*. 灌输;使渗透
2. auspicious / ɔːˈspɪʃəs/ *adj*. 有助于成功的;吉利的
3. homonym /ˈhɒmənɪm / *n*. 同音异义词
4. homophone /ˈhɒməfəʊn / *n*. 同音异形异义字
5. ingot /ˈɪŋgət / *n*. 锭;铸块
6. surplus /ˈsɜːpləs / *n*. 剩余;盈余,顺差

象征意义	**Symbolic Meanings**
富余	abundance / surplus
繁荣	prosperity
好运	good luck, good fortune
长寿	longevity
多子,生育能力	fertility
财富和力量	wealth and strength
和谐和繁荣	harmony and prosperity
全家团团圆圆	family unity, completeness and happiness
新的一年节节高	ladder-like ascent to new levels of glory in the coming new year
象征	symbolize
丰年	a plentiful year
年年高	improvement in life year by year
古代的金银锭	ancient gold and silver ingots
吉祥的	auspicious
充满了吉祥和象征意义	be imbued with auspicious and symbolic meanings
象征着好运	symbolize good luck
象征吉祥的果子	symbolize auspicious fruits
象征着子孙满堂	suggest / symbolize a family with a large number of children and grandchildren

Vocabulary

1. preliminary /prɪˈlɪmɪnəri/ *adj*. 初步的,预备的
2. scrub /skrʌb/ *v*. 擦洗,刷洗
3. narcissus /nɑːˈsɪsəs/ *n*. 水仙

节前准备	**Preparations for the Festival**
腊八节	Laba Festival
腊月	the twelfth lunar month
小年夜	preliminary eve
为了得到天赐的恩惠	win a little heavenly favor
除尘、洗涤和擦洗	dust, wash and scrub
来年收获满满,身体健康,吉祥如意	have a good harvest, good health, and good luck in the coming year
(春节)大扫除	spring cleaning
扫地	sweep the floor
拿起扫帚和簸箕	pick up the broom and dust pan
清洁衣服、床上用品和餐具	clean clothes, bedclothes and utensils
清偿债务	settle one's debts
扫除晦气	sweep away any ill fortune
迎接好运	make way for incoming good luck
逛大集	visit village fairs / open-air markets
购买新年探亲访友的礼物	buy gifts for the new year visits
摊贩	street vendor(s)
腊梅	wax plum
香气扑鼻的白色水仙	fragrant white narcissus
桃树	peach tree
季节性的最爱	seasonal favorite(s)

Vocabulary

1. décor /deɪˈkɔːr / *n*. 装饰，布置
2. vertical /ˈvɜːtɪk(ə)l/ *adj*. 垂直的；纵向的
3. horizontal /ˌhɒrɪˈzɒntl / *adj*. 水平的
4. ward off 避开，阻挡
5. livestock /ˈlaɪvstɒk / *n*. 牲畜，家畜

新年装饰	**New Year Decorations**
居家装饰品	home decoration
节日装饰	festive décor
在窗户上贴剪纸，贴窗花	paste paper-cuts on windows
彩色木刻版画	colorful woodblock print
神采奕奕的笑脸	healthy smiling
门神	door god
手写在红纸上的寓意吉祥的字	single auspicious characters handwritten on bright red paper
贴春联	paste spring couplets
年画	folk painting
横批	horizontal banner
对联（上联下联）	vertical paper banners
相辅相成的	complementary
孩童、荷花及葫芦图案	the child，lotus and bottle gourd designs
家禽、牲畜、水果、鱼	domestic birds，livestock，fruit，fish
质朴、豪放的风格	simple and bold style
色彩鲜艳	bright in color
精美细腻	delicate and fine
欢庆节日的气氛	an atmosphere of rejoicing and celebration
辟邪	ward off evil spirits and bad luck

Vocabulary

1. usher /ˈʌʃə(r) / *v*. 引导,引领
2. deprivation /ˌdeprɪˈveɪʃn / *n*. 贫困,匮乏
3. precinct /ˈpriːsɪŋkt / *n*. 管理区,管辖区
4. deafening /ˈdefnɪŋ / *adj*. 震耳欲聋的,极喧闹的
5. viewership / ˈvjuːərʃɪp / *n*. (电视节目的)观众;收视率

庆祝节日	**Celebrations and Festivities**
节日气氛	festive atmosphere
给人们带来欢乐	bring enjoyment to people
辞旧迎新	usher out the old year and welcome in the new
各地风俗传统不同	regional customs and traditions vary widely
每年一次的团圆宴	annual reunion dinner
最长的公共假期	the longest public holiday
春运	the Spring Festival Travel Rush
装扮	dress up
物质匮乏	material deprivation
放鞭炮	light / set off firecrackers
烧竹条	burn bamboo sticks
震耳欲聋的爆竹声	the deafening sounds of firecrackers
城区禁止燃放烟花爆竹	ban fireworks and firecrackers in certain precincts of cities
限制性燃放烟花爆竹	light firecrackers and launch fireworks in a limited scale
欢乐的夜晚	a night of merriment
驱邪	chase off the evil spirits
除夕	Chinese New Year's Eve
关门闭户驱鬼压邪	scare away evil spirits with the household doors sealed
团圆饭	family reunion dinner
央视春晚	CCTV Chinese New Year's Gala
以音乐、舞蹈、戏剧、喜剧为特色的综艺节目	feature a variety show of drama, dance, music and comedy
守岁	*shousui*; to keep awake the whole night and morning; to stay up late on New Year's Eve

为父母增寿	add on to one's parents' longevity
派发红包	to hand out red packets
红包	red envelopes stuffed with "lucky money", red packets
压岁钱	New Year's money
虚拟红包	virtual red envelopes
群发红包	distribute virtual red envelopes within group chats

Vocabulary

1. paternal / pə'tɜːrnl / *adj*. 父亲的;父系的
2. maternal / mə'tɜːrnl / *adj*. 母亲的;母系的
3. natal /'neɪtl / *adj*. 出生的;出生地的
4. pageantry / 'pædʒəntri / *n*. 壮丽,华丽

拜年	**New Year Visits**
交换礼物	exchange gifts
给家族长者拜年	visit the oldest and most senior members of the extended families
尊崇长者	honour and pay respect to the elders
互相串门	exchange visits
民间盛事	folk pageantry
父系的亲属	paternal families' relatives
外祖父母	maternal grandparents
原生家庭	natal family
大年初二,开年	"the beginning of the year", the second day of the Chinese New Year
(婚嫁的女儿)回娘家拜年	(married daughters) to visit their birth parents, relatives and close friends

Vocabulary

1. ancestral /æn'sestrəl / *adj*. 祖先的;祖传的
2. incense /'ɪnsens / *n*. 香;焚香时的烟,香气
3. tablet / 'tæblət / *n*. (用于刻字的)牌,碑,匾
4. kowtow / ˌkaʊ'taʊ / *v*. 叩头

祭祀仪式	**Sacrifice Rituals**
祭拜祖先	pay respect to the ancestors
迎天上地下的各路神仙	welcome the deities of the heavens and earth
迎财神	welcome the god of wealth
最受尊崇的神	the most worshipped deity
祭祀各路神仙和祖先	offer sacrifices to various deities and to the ancestors
烧香	burn incense
祖先牌位	ancestral tablet
宗祠;祠堂	ancestral hall
磕头	kowtow
去寺庙祈祷来年的好运和健康	go to the temples to pray for good fortune and health in the coming year
财神到!	The god of wealth has come!

Vocabulary

1. glutinous /ˈgluːtənəs / *adj*. 黏的;胶质的
2. acrobatic /ˌækrəˈbætɪk / *adj*. 杂技的,特技的
3. parade / pəˈreɪd / *n*. 游行;列队表演,展示
4. troupe / truːp / *n*. 巡回演出团
5. stilt / stɪlt / *n*. 高跷

元宵节	**Lantern Festival**
标志着中国新年的结束	mark the end of the Chinese Spring Festival period
农历的第一个月圆之夜	the first full moon night in the Chinese calendar
中国的情人节	China's Valentine's Day
放鞭炮	set off fireworks
节日游行	festive parade
赏月	appreciate the bright full moon
吃元宵	eat rice dumplings (a sweet glutinous rice ball brewed in a soup)
敲鼓	sound a drum
深受社会各阶层的欢迎	be popular among all social strata
舞龙	dragon dance

舞狮队	lion dance troupe
中国传统民间舞蹈	traditional folk dances in China
追溯到三国时期	date back to the Three Kingdoms Period (220-280)
勇敢和力量的象征	a symbol of bravery and strength
训练有素的表演者	highly-trained performer
穿着狮子服	be in a lion suit
随着鼓、锣和钹的节拍跳舞	dance to the beat of a drum, gong and cymbals
杂技	acrobats
杂技团	acrobatic troupe
踩高跷	walk on stilts
重新营业	reopen businesses
学校开学	(schools) back in session

Vocabulary

1. riddle / ˈrɪdl / *n*. 谜语
2. pastime / ˈpæstaɪm / *n*. 娱乐，消遣
3. floating / ˈfləʊtɪŋ / *adj*. 漂浮的，浮动的

赏灯	**Appreciation of Lanterns**
点亮灯笼	light lanterns
漂浮的、固定的、手持的和飞翔的灯笼	floating, fixed, held, and flying lanterns
各种形状和大小的灯笼	lanterns of various shapes and sizes
传统的中国形象和符号	traditional Chinese images and symbols
吸引众多观众	attract numerous viewers
在悬挂的灯笼下散步	walk under a hanging lantern
屋外点蜡烛	light candles outside houses
提着灯笼到街上走	walk the street carrying lighted lantern
放飞天灯	send up flying lanterns
节日的消遣方式	festival pastime
猜灯谜	guess / solve lantern riddles
把纸条贴在五彩缤纷的灯笼上	paste the riddles on colorful lanterns
扯下谜语	pull the riddle off
找灯笼主人核对答案	go to the lantern owner to check the answer

A3. Speaking Activities

Situational Speech

The International Students Association of XXX University is about to hold a seminar on Chinese culture. You are invited to deliver a speech in the seminar, introducing briefly to international students **the Chinese New Year celebrations and traditions in your hometown.** Prepare a speech of about 5 minutes. Your speech might cover:

- Local legends about the Chinese New Year.
- Preparations for the Chinese New Year.
- Festivities and celebrations of the Chinese New Year.
- The significance of the Chinese New Year to people in your hometown.

You may refer to the words and expressions in Part A, but don't confine yourself to them.

Role Play

Chinese New Year celebrations may vary from region to region, village to village, and even family to family. A TV station with a large international viewership is making a featured program to introduce different traditions and celebrations of Chinese New Year in different parts of China. As journalists of this program, you and your colleagues need to **interview at least 5 students** about the unique customs of New Year celebration in their hometown. Your questions might include:

- What are the typical foods on the reunion table? Why?
- Do people offer sacrifices to gods and their own ancestors? How?
- What is the first thing people do on the first day of the New Year?
- How do people greet each other?
- When and how do people pay New Year visits to friends and relatives?

After the interview, summarize the different traditions in different places of China and broadcast to the international viewers.

Read and Share

Read the following paragraphs about **taboos** around the Spring Festival and share your views.

Paragraph 1

In addition to red envelopes, which are usually given from older people to younger people, small gifts (usually food or sweets) are also exchanged between friends or relatives (of different households) during Chinese New Year. Gifts are usually brought when visiting friends or relatives at their homes. Common gifts include fruits (typically oranges, but never trade pears), cakes, biscuits, chocolates, and candies. Gifts are preferred to be wrapped with red or golden paper, which symbolizes good luck. Certain items should not be given, as they are considered taboo. Taboo gifts include items associated with funerals (e.g., handkerchiefs, towels, chrysanthemums, items colored white and black), items that show that time is running out (e.g., clocks and watches), sharp objects that symbolize cutting a tie (e.g., scissors and knives) and items that symbolize that you want to walk away from a relationship (e.g., shoes and sandals).

(Adapted from *Chinatravel.com*)

Paragraph 2

Just as use of lucky words and actions are encouraged at this time, so are there taboos. It is important, for instance, to avoid the number "four" (si), because it sounds like the word for death; any words and their homonyms related to death, illness, or bankruptcy are inauspicious. Kitchen work and sewing are avoided because use of knives, scissors, needles, and other sharp objects is strictly discouraged. Traditionally, one did not pick up a broom on New Year's Day for fear of accidentally sweeping good luck out the door, and even the sight of one might portend a year full of housekeeping drudgery.

(Adapted from *Columbia.edu*)

Ideas for Sharing:

- What are the taboos around the Spring Festival in your hometown?
- Does your family observe these taboos? Why?

Debate

Sending greetings through WeChat or other social media gradually becomes the most popular way to greet people during Chinese New Year. Greetings with text and graphics by smart phone is vivid and convenient. Even a friend is far away from you, he or she can still receive congratulations immediately. Besides, virtual red packet makes a lot of people happy. No matter how much money they can receive, people still enjoy it.

(Adapted from *topchinatravel.com*)

Topic for Debate:

Greetings through social media could replace face-to-face greetings.

Interpretation

Interpret the paragraphs below into English with the words and expressions you learned in Part A.

Paragraph 1

春节是中国人最重要的节日,春节是全家团圆的节日。中国有56个民族,少数民族与汉族人几乎在同一天庆祝春节,但各个民族的习俗有所不同。每年腊月二十之后开始进入全年交通最繁忙的"春运",机场、火车站和长途汽车站挤满了要回家过年的人。春节正值农历正月初一,通常比公历晚一个月。严格来说,春节每年从农历十二月初开始,一直持续到次年农历一月中旬。春节期间有许多习俗,有些今天仍然流行,有些已经渐渐被人忘记了。

Paragraph 2

农历腊月二十三是"小年"。小年之后,人们开始为即将到来的新年做准备。首先,要采购年货,包括各种肉类、水果、糖果和坚果。其次,还要准备各种装饰品,比如年画、春联等,以及孩子们的新衣服和鞋子。春节前另外一项重要的活动是"大扫除"。一般都是全家总动员,彻底打扫屋内屋外,扫地拖地、擦玻璃、洗涤衣物和床上用品以及各种餐具厨具等,直到各个房间都纤尘不染。人们会用大红的春联、窗花以及鲜艳的年画装饰门窗,营造出欢乐喜庆的氛围。有意思的是,福字在很多地方是要倒着贴的,这寓意着"福到了"。

Paragraph 3

燃放烟花爆竹曾经是春节最典型的习俗。人们认为这种噼噼啪啪的声音可以辟邪。现在,由于安全、噪音和污染等,很多大城市都禁止燃放烟花爆竹。尽管如此,热闹的气氛不仅充斥着每家每户,而且渗透大街小巷。舞狮舞龙、庙会等一系列活动持续多天。随着元宵节的到来,春节也就结束了。

A4. Culture Highlights

Q: *Most westerners prefer trimmed meat and filleted fish, while throughout most of China, fish is cooked and served whole with intact head and tail, especially on dinner tables during Chinese New Year. Why?*

A: Food not only serves as the source of nutrition for humans, but also plays various roles in our daily life, beliefs and society. In Chinese culture, foods have always been used as **symbols of meaning** in many occasions, to impart different information. Whole fish symbolizes abundance, and so for special occasions like weddings and birthdays, it is customary and good luck to serve a whole fish at the table. Whole steamed fish with scallions, shiitakes and cilantro is classic in China.

Food not only expresses but also **establishes the relationship** between people and their environment as well as between people and what they believe. When friends or relatives visit, people usually treat them with fish to show respect and enhance friendship. It is customary to serve the whole fish last, pointed toward the guest of honor at the table. The fish is never completely eaten, as leaving a little bit of it represents the family's ability to "always have enough." The most-esteemed part of the fish, the head, is saved for the most-esteemed guest at the table. Being offered the head of the fish is a show of respect, because that is the most-prized and the most-flavorful part of the fish.

(Adapted from *cookingchanneltv.com*)

Q: *People say Lantern Festival is the Chinese equivalent to Valentine's Day. Why?*
A: The history of the Lantern Festival could be traced back to the Han Dynasty (202 BC-220 AD), and from the very beginning, lanterns have been an indispensable part of the day. Even though most Chinese dynasties had curfews during the night, all the people were allowed to stay out on the days around the Lantern Festival. The Chinese women, who had to stay indoors for most of their lives, were permitted to **admire the lanterns and the full moon** on the day as well. Therefore, it was almost the only time for young men and women to meet with each other and fall in love. The other evidence of the Lantern Festival being Chinese Valentine's Day is recorded in **Chinese literature.** In the thousands of ancient poems passed on from the Tang and Song dynasties, many depicted ardent love for their partners. The festive atmosphere, the performances, and the moonlight jointly created **the best time for a date.** With lanterns as the set and the moon in the sky, the night could be turned into a stage for the best possible romance.

Compared to the Qixi Festival on the seventh day of the seventh lunar month, which is more widely recognized by young couples and commercial brands, the Lantern Festival has a relatively low profile. But it is undeniable that in Chinese history, it is indeed a day for love. That's why it is called by some as the Chinese equivalent to Valentine's Day.

(Adapted from *visitingbeijing.com.cn*)

Q: *In traditional Chinese culture, there are 12 zodiac signs. In Western astrology, there are also 12 zodiac signs. Are they the same? If not, what are the major differences?*

A: There are the same number of signs in both Chinese culture and Western culture. The Chinese signs are: Rat, Ox, Tiger, Rabbit, Dragon, Snake, Horse, Goat, Monkey, Rooster, Dog, and Pig. The Western signs are: Ram, Bull, Twins, Crab, Lion, Virgin, Scales, Scorpion, Centaur, Sea-Goat, Water Bearer, and Fish.

Two are superficially similar: Ox/Bull and Goat/Ram. However, there are more differences than similarities between the two systems.

- **Timeframe.** Chinese zodiac signs are divided by years, whereas western ones are divided by months.
- **Origin.** In Chinese culture, the 12 signs are derived from a myth that when the Jade Emperor was developing a calendar, all creatures on Earth were summoned to participate in a race. The first 12 to cross the line were awarded signs in the Chinese zodiac. This differs from Western astrology where the 12 signs are based on constellations' positions relative to the earth. The constellations were named according to Greek mythology.
- **Lunar vs. solar calendars.** Chinese zodiac is based on the lunar calendar, which is arranged by the phases of the Moon, whereas Western zodiac is based on the Earth's orbit around the sun (and resulting celestial alignment), which gives every zodiac month a set date, lasting between 29 and 31 days. This is why Western zodiac star signs are also known as sun signs.
- **The elements.** The Chinese astrology system identifies five elements: fire, earth, metal, water, and wood. Because the animals are on 12-year cycles and there are five elements, the entire Chinese zodiac-element cycle lasts 60 years. In this system, each sign has a fire, earth, metal, water, and wood variety depending on the birth year. In the Western system, only four elements are identified: fire, earth, air, and water, and each element is associated with three signs with psychological features.
- **Lunar phases and nodes.** Chinese astrology places emphasis on the lunar phase at the time of birth. There are four moon phases: new moon, waxing moon, full moon, and waning moon. The Western system, comparatively, considers two moon nodes; the North or Ascending Node, and the South or Descending Node.

(Adapted from *Chinahighlights.com*)

A5. Extension

Synonym Discrimination

Can you figure out the differences among the words and phrases below?

Group 1: vacation / festival / holiday / carnival

Group 2: folklore / tale / myth / mythology / legend / epic / fable

Extensive Reading

The Chinese Calendar

The marking of the passage of time in China has for millennia been closely linked to the cyclical pattern of agricultural production. The vast majority of the population of this agrarian society has always resided in rural areas and supported itself directly or indirectly by the tilling of the soil. One's activities were arranged around events necessary to sustain life: plowing the fields, sowing seed, nurturing the crops, and gathering the harvest. As such it was necessary to be able to keep track of the optimal times for performing certain tasks. If a peasant waited too long to plant a crop, he might miss advantageous spring rains; if he hesitated to reap his more delicate vegetables, he might lose them to the first frost.

It was from this necessity that the Chinese lunar calendar was born; and it is this calendar which fixes the dates of the lunar new year and other events related to the holiday season.

Known as both the agricultural calendar and the old calendar, the lunar calendar is also referred to as the Xia calendar because legend holds that it dates from the time of the Xia dynasty (21st to 16th centuries BCE). No sophisticated astronomical instruments were necessary to observe the regular waxing and waning of the moon, and so it is the earth's satellite itself that is considered to be the earliest instrument of celestial observation. Peasants could measure time by simply recording the revolutions and phases of the moon. While useful for counting time periods, it wasn't much help in accurately predicting seasonal changes. The ancients knew that there were roughly 29.5 days between new moons and that therefore 12 revolutions of the moon required 354 days. While this was relatively close to the time required for the earth to make one turn around the sun (365.25 days) and thus for the seasons to complete one full cycle, it was a great enough difference to render the lunar calendar impractical for foretelling seasonal changes. The same date on a calendar of 12 lunar months would fall at a different seasonal time each year.

To account for the extra half day in each lunar revolution, the calendar makers assigned 29 days to half the months and 30 to the others. To reconcile the differences in lunar measurement with the solar year of four full seasons, one intercalary, or extra month was added every two or three years. The result was a luni-solar calendar that, in each 19-year period, has 12 years with 12 months and seven with 13 months. Oracle bone inscriptions of the Shang dynasty (ca. 1600 to ca. 1050 BCE) offer evidence that the intercalary month had already been adopted by that time.

By the Qin dynasty (221 to 206 BCE) the calendar had been further divided into 24 periods of 15 days each. These are referred to as solar and mid-solar terms, and each is named in accordance with corresponding seasonal changes (e.g., "Waking of Insects," "Grain Rain," "Great Heat," "Frost's Descent," etc.). The beginning date of each solar and mid-solar term is determined by the position of the sun in one of the 12 signs of the zodiac, which in Chinese are represented by animals (e.g., rat, ox, tiger, rabbit).

In 104 BCE Emperor Wu of the Han dynasty (206 BCE to 220 CE) approved a calendar reform that fixed the beginning of the year on the day of the first new moon after the sun enters the 11th sign of the solar zodiac, or the second new moon after the winter solstice. This is also the first day of the solar term known as "beginning of spring." For centuries the festival observing the first day of the year was popularly called (lunar) New Year's Day, or literally, "First morning of the year" (*yuan dan*), "Beginning of the first month" (*yuan zheng*), or "First day" (*yuan ri*). When the Republic of China was founded in 1912, the government officially adopted the Gregorian calendar as the "public calendar," and recognition of January 1 as the first day of the new year. Since that time lunar New Year's Day has been commonly known as "Spring Festival." The old lunar calendar continues to be used popularly in conjunction with the solar-oriented Gregorian calendar as a way of marking traditional observances, the dates of which, like Spring Festival, are dependent on its calculations, and which are closely associated with its agrarian origins.

(Adapted from *columbia.edu*)

Chinese New Year Firecrackers

It is an important custom to set off firecrackers and fireworks during the Chinese New Year period. Chinese New Year celebrations would not be complete without them.

Why light firecrackers on Chinese New Year?

In traditional Chinese culture, firecrackers were originally used to scare away evil spirits. As the legend goes, a monster called Nian would come out to eat villagers and destroy their houses on each New Year's Eve. The villagers discovered that burning dry bamboo to produce an explosive sound scared away the monster. Since then, it has become a tradition for Chinese New Year. Today, lighting firecrackers and fireworks is a major custom to celebrate the coming of the New Year, and also a way to enhance the festive atmosphere. So, even though lighting firecrackers produces a loud noise nuisance and piles of red paper shreds, Chinese people not only take it in their stride, but also they generally enjoy firecrackers.

The history of firecrackers

In the Tang Dynasty (618-907), gunpowder was discovered by chance, which led to the invention of firecrackers in China. People found that a loud blast could be produced by inserting gunpowder into the hollow of a bamboo stick and then throwing it into a fire. The first firecrackers were born. In the Song Dynasty (960-1279), paper tubes came to replace the bamboo stalks. Wrapped in red, a lucky color for Chinese, firecrackers became increasingly popular to enhance celebrations and religious ceremonies. The red paper is left around (for at least a day) after letting off firecrackers, so as not to "sweep away good luck".

Setting off firecrackers during Chinese New Year

It is a countrywide tradition to set off firecrackers during the Chinese New Year period. But the time to set them off differs from region to region. It is popular to set off firecrackers at the following times:

The moment the new year arrives, there is a cacophony of fireworks and firecrackers all around, accompanied by thick smoke, the shaking of buildings, and the noise of hundreds of car alarms. In large cities, fireworks are set off continuously for one to two hours.

Before New Year's Eve dinner. When the reunion dinner is ready, many families light firecrackers to invite ancestors to celebrate the festival together. It is also a way to add a jubilant atmosphere to the festival and it brings great happiness.

At the stroke of midnight on New Year's Day. It is customary to stay up until midnight after the reunion dinner. Firecrackers and fireworks are set off at the stroke of midnight to scare away evil spirits and celebrate the coming of the new year.

On New Year's Day morning. In some places, families first set off firecrackers when they open the door or before they go out. It symbolizes good luck throughout the whole year. Many families will not sweep the red paper left by firecrackers immediately because they believe that the act of sweeping on this day is associated with sweeping wealth away.

The Lantern Festival. It marks the end of the celebration of Chinese New Year. People set off firecrackers and fireworks to ward off misfortune and bring good luck.

Other occasions to light firecrackers

Firecrackers are commonly used in celebrations of holidays or festivals. There are many other occasions where firecrackers are used, such as wedding ceremonies, seniors' birthday parties, house warming parties, and the opening of a business. They are used to bring blessings and happiness. Setting off firecrackers is not always used for celebrations. In the Qingming Festival and at funerals, the use of firecrackers is to honor the dead.

Bans or restrictions on firecrackers and fireworks

For the sake of safety and environmental protection, many cities across China have imposed bans or restrictions on the use of fireworks and firecrackers during festivals and holidays. In these cases, it's illegal for individuals to set off fireworks and firecrackers. People can only set them off at designated venues. If you would like to see a show of firecrackers and fireworks in a city, you need to check the designated venues and time frames in advance.

(Adapted from *chinahighlights.com*)

A6. Assignment

Poster Design

Form groups of 3 or 4 and **design an English poster** featuring the Chinese New Year. You need to

- Discuss what festival elements or words should be included.
- Design the layout of the festival elements and words.
- Print and share the poster with your classmates.
- Explain the design process on class.

Part B Other Festivals

B1. Introduction

Legends of the Dragon Boat Festival

Beginning on the fifth day of the fifth lunar month, people of several ethnic groups throughout China and the world celebrate the Dragon Boat festival, especially in the middle and lower reaches of the Yangtze River. The Dragon Boat Festival was originally selected into the first batch of National Intangible Cultural Heritage items on May 20th, 2006. On October 30th, 2009, it was added to the UNESCO Representative List of the Intangible Cultural Heritage of Humanity. Almost every Chinese knows some stories about Dragon Boat Festival, which shows that this traditional festival had firmly rooted in people's mind. There are numerous versions of the festival's origin, among which three legends are the most widely circulated.

The legend of Qu Yuan, a famous patriotic poet

This is the best known legend in China. According to history record, Qu Yuan was an official of the Chu State. Being the most talented poet of his time, Qu Yuan left us "Lisao, Suffering Throes", the most beautiful poem of all time. He dedicated his whole life in helping the king to build his motherland stronger, but the king believed in slanders and punish Qu Yuan severely. On 278 BC, the Chu State was invaded by another state, which was excruciating to Qu Yuan. Though heartbroken to see his country being intruded, Qu Yuan never abandoned his faith and country. On the fifth day of the fifth lunar month, after writing down his last poem, Qu Yuan drowned himself in Miluo River (a branch of Yangtze River) as a gesture of dying along with his motherland. After his tragic death, the Chu State was shadowed with grief. The fishmen rowed along the river to find his body, while one of them took out some cooked rice ball, throwing them into the water. He explained that as long as the fish were fed, they would not bite Mr. Qu's body. People in the area all followed this example. Gradually rowing developed into dragon boat racing and rice balls became *tzung tzu* (or *zongzi*, glutinous rice wrapped in a pyramid shape using bamboo or reed leaves) and passed down from generation to generation as a Chinese tradition.

The legend of Wu Zixu, a capable court minister

In Jiangsu and Zhejiang, this legend is quite popular. Wu Zixu, just like Qu Yuan, was from the Chu State 2000 years ago. His father was once the royal tutor but the king, misled by false reports of rebellion plots, ordered the execution of him and Wu Zixu's older brother. Struck by sorrow, Wu later moved to another the state of Wu to help them conquer Chu for revenge. His assistance laid the cornerstone of the accomplishment achieved by the state of Wu. Yet again he was entrapped by bad guys and was then forced to commit suicide on the fifth day of the fifth lunar month. He died with sorrow and anguish, and the locals sympathize with him. A series of activities were held to commemorate his tragic death.

The legend of Cao E, a filial dutiful daughter

According to legend, Cao E, from Zhejiang, lived in Eastern Han dynasty (23-220 A.D.). Her father drowned in the river and his body could not be found for days while

Cao E was only 14 years old. She loved her father so much that she believed it was her duty to find his body and give him a decent funeral. She walked along the bank day and night, searching and crying her heart out. Seventeen days later, on the fifth day of the fifth lunar month, she jumped into the water too. Miraculously, she came back to life with her father's body in her arms. People all said that the heaven was moved by her filial affection. To salute her, people built up temples for her, and celebrated Dragon Boat Festival ever after.

The festivities vary from region to region, but they usually share several features. A memorial ceremony offering sacrifices to a local hero is combined with sporting events such as dragon races, dragon boating and willow shooting, feasts of rice dumplings, eggs and ruby sulphur wine, and folk entertainments including opera, song and unicorn dances. Participants also ward off evil during the festival by bathing in flower-scented water, wearing five-colour silk, hanging plants such as moxa and calamus over their doors, and pasting paper cut-outs in their windows. The Dragon Boat Festival strengthens bonds within families and establishes a harmonious relationship between humanity and nature. It also encourages the expression of imagination and creativity, contributing to a vivid sense of cultural identity.

(Adapted from *chinaculture.org.*, *chinahighlights.com* & *UNESCO.org*)

The Mid-Autumn Festival: Celebrations

The Mid-Autumn Festival is also called the Moon Festival or the Mooncake Festival. It traditionally falls on the 15th day of the eighth month of the Chinese lunar calendar, which is in September or early October on the Gregorian calendar. It is the second most important festival in China after Chinese New Year. Chinese people celebrate it by gathering for dinners, worshiping the moon, lighting paper lanterns, eating mooncakes, etc.

Enjoying family reunions

The roundness of the moon represents the reunion of the family in Chinese minds. Families will have dinner together on the evening of the Mid-Autumn Festival. The public holiday (usually 3 days) is mainly for Chinese people working in different places to have enough time to reunite. Those staying too far away from their parents' home usually get together with friends.

Eating mooncakes

Mooncakes are the most representative food for the Mid-Autumn Festival, because of their round shape and sweet flavor. Family members usually gather round and cut a mooncake into pieces and share its sweetness. Nowadays, mooncakes are made in various shapes (round, square, heart-shaped, animal-shaped...) and in various flavors, which make them more attractive and enjoyable for a variety of consumers. In some shopping malls, super big mooncakes may be displayed to attract customers.

Appreciating the moon

The full moon is the symbol of family reunions in Chinese culture. It is said, sentimentally, that "the moon on the night of Mid-Autumn Festival is the brightest and the most beautiful". Chinese people usually set a table outside their houses and sit together to admire the full moon while enjoying tasty mooncakes. Parents with little kids often tell the legend of Chang'e Flying to the Moon. As a game, kids try their best to find the shape of Chang'e on the moon. There are many Chinese poems praising the beauties of the moon and expressing people's longing for their friends and families at Mid-Autumn.

Worshiping the moon

According to the legend of Mid-Autumn Festival, a fairy maiden named Chang'e lives on the moon with a cute rabbit. On the night of the Mid-Autumn Festival, people set a table under the moon with mooncakes, snacks, fruits, and a pair of candles lit on it. Some believe that by worshiping the moon, Chang'e (the moon goddess) may fulfill their wishes.

In modern times, besides the traditional activities, many Chinese people send WeChat red envelopes and / or go traveling during the 3-day public holiday to celebrate the festival. Besides the above common celebrations, different regions also have some unique traditions. For example, in Hong Kong, an annual fire dragon show is held in the Tai Hang neighborhood during Mid-Autumn Festival.

The Mid-Autumn Festival is also widely celebrated in many Asian communities besides China. Many interesting activities with unique local features are held. In Singapore, Malaysia, and the Philippines — three countries with many ethnic Chinese citizens — the celebrations are more Chinese, such as lighting lanterns and dragon dances. The date is also the same as in China. In other countries, such as Japan, South Korea, and Vietnam, which have also been influenced deeply by Chinese culture, new celebrations have been derived from their unique cultures.

(Adapted from *chinahighlights.com*)

B2. Words and Expressions

Vocabulary

1. ground / graʊnd / *adj*. 切碎的,磨碎的
2. repellant / rɪˈpelənt / *n*. 驱虫剂
3. herb / hɜːb / *n*. 药草;香草;草本植物
4. perfume /ˈpɜːfjuːm / *n*. 香水;香料

二月二	**Longtaitou Festival / Dragon Heads Raising Festival**
农耕文化	agrarian Chinese culture
万物之王	the king of all creatures
人类的祖先	the ancestor of human beings
吃春饼	eat Chinese pancakes
香囊,香袋	perfume bag
香料粉末	powder of ground fragrant herbs
驱虫剂	insect repellant
太昊陵庙会	Taihao temple fair
祖先的神灵伏羲和女娲	ancestral deities Fuxi and Nüwa
理发	go to the barber
吃龙食	eat "dragon" food
炒豆子	fried beans
龙须(面条)	dragon's beard (noodles)
龙耳(饺子)	dragon's ears (dumplings)
龙鳞(春卷)	dragon's scales (spring rolls)
龙籽(爆米花)	dragon seeds (popcorn)

Vocabulary

1. sacrifice / ˈsækrɪfaɪs / *n*. 牺牲;供奉;献祭
2. ancestral / ænˈsestrəl / *adj*. 祖先的,祖传的
3. cemetery / ˈseməteri / *n*. 公墓,墓地
4. condolence / kənˈdəʊləns / *n*. 吊唁,哀悼
5. martyr /ˈmaːrtər / *n*. 烈士
6. exile / ˈeksaɪl / *n*. 流放;被流放者

清明节	**Qingming Festival / Tomb-Sweeping Festival**
祭祀节日	day of sacrifice
祭拜祖先	commemorate and pay respect to one's ancestors
祭祖	offer sacrifices to ancestors
哀悼仪式	mourning ceremony
哀悼之情	condolence
扫墓的人	tomb sweeper
参观清理墓地	visit and clean the gravesite / cemeteries
去乡间散步	go for walks in the countryside
种柳树	plant willows
放风筝	fly kites / kite flying
烈士陵园	martyrs park
纪念碑	memorial tablet
向革命烈士致敬	pay homage to revolutionary martyrs
寒食节	Hanshi Festival / Cold Food Festival / Smoke-Banning Festival
忠臣	a loyal minister / court official
春秋时期	the Spring and Autumn Period
流放	be in exile
清明	Pure Brightness
踏青节	Taqing Festival
踏青，春游	spring outing
清除墓地上的杂草	remove the weeds from the gravesite
添新土	add new earth
把柳树枝放在墓地顶上	place willow branches atop the gravesite
门旁插柳	willow branches inserted on each gate
殡葬用品	funeral supplies / products
纸钱	hell notes / joss paper
祭祀用香	joss stick
焚香	burn incense
在墓前放置祭品和纸钱	place an offering of food and paper money at the tomb
在祖先祭坛前祭祀	making offerings at ancestral altars
向烈士敬献花圈和鲜花	place wreaths and flowers at martyrs' shrines

Vocabulary

1. pyramidal / ˈpɪrəmɪdl / *adj*. 锥体的,金字塔形的
2. realgar /rɪˈælgər / *n*. 雄黄
3. ferment / fəˈment / *v*. (使)发酵
4. mugwort / ˈmʌgwɜːt / *n*. 艾蒿
5. calamus / ˈkæləməs / *n*. 菖蒲
6. prevalent / ˈprevələnt / *adj*. 盛行的,普遍的
7. synchronicity / ˌsɪŋkrəˈnɪsəti / *n*. 同步性,同时发生

端午节	**Dragon Boat Festival**
吃粽子	eat sticky rice dumplings (*zongzi*)
用糯米做成的粽子	dumpling made of glutinous rice
肉、豆子和其他馅料	meats, beans, and other fillings
三角形或矩形	triangle or rectangle shape
锥体形	pyramidal shape
用竹叶或芦苇叶包裹	wrap in bamboo or reed leaves
用浸湿的茎秆捆扎	tie with soaked stalks
彩色丝绳	colorful silky cords
喝雄黄酒	drink realgar wine
驱除疾病和邪恶	drive diseases and evils away
杀虫驱邪	kill insects and drive away evil spirits
发酵的谷物	fermented cereals
雄黄粉	powdered realgar
佩戴香囊	wear perfume pouches
用彩色丝绸缝制小袋子	sew little bags with colorful silk cloth
在袋子里装满香料或草药	fill the bags with perfumes or herbal medicines
用丝线把袋子串起来	string the bags with silk threads
挂在孩子的脖子上	hang around kids' necks
系在胸前作为装饰品	tie to the front of a garment as an ornament
挂艾蒿和菖蒲	hang Chinese mugwort and calamus
疾病多发的时节	a time when diseases are more prevalent
药用	medicinal effect
阻止苍蝇和蚊子	deter flies and mosquitoes
水生植物	aquatic plant

门过梁，门楣	doors lintels
龙舟竞渡，赛龙舟	dragon boat racing
设定节奏	set a pace
引导划桨者的动作	guide the paddlers' move
频率和同步	the frequency and synchronicity
动作和谐地划船	paddle harmoniously
同步用力	synchronized efforts
屈原（战国时期楚国人）	Qu Yuan (343-278 BC), a Chu State official in the Warring States Period
爱国诗人	patriotic poet
国际盛事，国际竞赛	international event
用龙翘起的头和尾装饰	decorate with dragon's turnup head and tails
用传统吉祥图案雕刻或绘画	carve or paint with traditional auspicious patterns

Vocabulary

1. ill-fated /ˌɪlˈfeɪtɪd / *adj*. 不幸的，时运不济的
2. intangible / ɪnˈtændʒəbl / *adj*. 不可捉摸的；无形的
3. dexterity / dekˈsterəti / *n*. 灵巧，敏捷，机敏
4. celestial / səˈlestiəl / *adj*. 天空的，天上的
5. magpie / ˈmægpaɪ / *n*. 鹊，喜鹊

七夕节	**Qixi Festival / Double-Seventh Festival**
浪漫的传说	romantic legend
不幸的爱情	ill-fated love affair
织女	Zhinü, the weaver girl / a weaving girl / a weaver fairy
编织天空的彩霞	weave rosy clouds in the sky
厌烦了单调的神仙生活	get tired of the boring immortal life
下凡	descend to the mortal world
牛郎	Niulang, the cowherd / ox youth
王母娘娘	the Goddess of Heaven
凡人	mortal
天兵天将	celestial soldiers and generals
把织女带回天上	bring Zhinü back to heaven

牛皮	ox's hide
银河	river of stars, the Milky Way
鹊桥	magpie bridge
国家非物质文化遗产	the National Intangible Cultural Heritage
展示灵巧手艺	demonstrate dexterity
乞巧	plead skills
乞巧节	the Begging Festival
在月光下迅速地穿针	speedily thread a needle under moonlight
在瓜皮上雕刻奇异的花朵、动物和奇特的禽鸟	carve exotic flowers, animals and unusual birds on a melon skin
敬拜织女(织女星)	worship the weaver fairy (the star Vega)
一桌供品	a table of offerings
展示自己的针线活	display one's needlework
祈祷收获忠贞的爱情	pray to find one's faithful lover
读诗至深夜	read poems until midnight
为了纪念传说中的牛	honour the legendary ox
摘几束野花挂在牛角上	pick bunches of wild flowers and hang them on the horns of oxen
巧果(各种形状的油炸面点)	skill fruit, fried pastries of different shapes
给心爱的人送花、巧克力和其他礼物	give flowers, chocolates and other presents to one's sweetheart
晚餐约会	dinner date
交换礼物	exchange gifts
表达爱意	express one's affection
恩爱情侣	lovebird
商业化	commercialize
排长队	long queue
登记结婚	register for marriage

Vocabulary

1. simultaneously / ˌsaɪmlˈteɪniəsli / *adv.* 同时地
2. scorch / skɔːtʃ / *v.* 烧焦,枯萎
3. crust / krʌst / *n.* (馅饼或比萨饼等的)酥皮;硬外皮
4. pomegranate / ˈpɑːmɪɡrænɪt / *n.* 石榴

中秋节	**Mid-Autumn Festival / Moon Festival / Mooncake Festival**
关于后羿和嫦娥的传说	the legend about Hou Yi and Chang'e
嫦娥奔月的传说	the legend of Chang E Flying to the Moon
伟大的射手	great archer
射下九个太阳	shoot down nine suns
飞上月亮	ascend to the moon
玉兔	jade rabbit
敬拜秋月	worship the harvest moon in autumn
为来年带来丰收	bring a plentiful harvest the following year
向月亮献祭	offer sacrifices to the moon
祭拜月亮女神	worship the moon goddess
阖家欢聚	enjoy family reunion
吃月饼	eat mooncakes
圆形	round shape
薄皮	thin crust
味甘,味甜	sweet flavor
把月饼切成块,分享它的甜蜜	cut a mooncake into pieces and share its sweetness
各种形状和口味	various shapes and flavors
对不同的消费者具有吸引力	be attractive for a variety of consumers
最传统的经典风味	the most traditional classic flavor
五仁	five kernels
混合坚果(杏仁、核桃、瓜子、芝麻、南瓜子)	mixed nuts (almonds, walnuts, dried melon seeds, sesame, and pumpkin seeds)
红豆沙	red bean paste
莲蓉	lotus seed paste
白芸豆沙	white kidney bean paste
鸭蛋黄	duck egg yolk
叉烧肉	roast pork
雪皮月饼	snow skin mooncake (a type of non-baked mooncake)
冻糯米皮	frozen glutinous rice crust
团圆和幸福的象征	a symbol of reunion and happiness
新鲜的大闸蟹	fresh hairy crab
石榴	pomegranate
但愿人长久,千里共婵娟。	Wish us a long life to share the graceful moonlight, though hundreds of miles apart.

Vocabulary

1. deprivation / ˌdeprɪˈveɪʃn / *n.* 贫困,匮乏
2. precinct / ˈpriːsɪŋkt / *n.* 管理区,管辖区
3. deafening / ˈdefnɪŋ / *adj.* 震耳欲聋的,极喧闹的
4. viewership / ˈvjuːərʃɪp / *n.* (电视节目的)观众;收视率

重阳节	**Chongyang Festival / Double Ninth Festival / Mountain-climbing Festival**
《易经》	*Yi Jing*, *The Book of Changes*
阴字	a *Yin* character, a feminine or negative character
阳字	a *Yang* character, a masculine or positive character
戴茱萸	wear *zhuyu* or cornel twigs (dogwood)
常青乔木	species of evergreen arbor
具有浓香的植物	heavy-scented plant
驱逐昆虫	expel insects
祛除湿气	get rid of the humidity
助消化	help digestion
清内热	cure inner heat
赏菊	enjoy chrysanthemum flowers
长寿花	flower of longevity
菊花展	chrysanthemum displays
将菊花贴在门窗上以"祛霉引吉"	stick chrysanthemums on doors and windows to "get rid of the bad luck and bring in the good ones"
将菊花插在头上的习俗	the custom of wearing chrysanthemum on people's heads
诗歌创作比赛	poem-composing competition
吃重阳糕	eat Chongyang cake
九层塔状糕点	nine-layer cake shaped like a tower
菊花糕	chrysanthemum cake or flower cake
菊花酒	chrysanthemum flower wine
庆祝丰收	celebrate crop harvests
有益健康	wholesome effects
缓解头痛	alleviate headache
控制体重	reduce weight
消除胃病	remove stomach trouble

疏解疼痛	assuagement of pain
调节体内能量的流动	regulation of the flow of vital energy
登高,爬山	ascend / climb heights or mountains
观光	go sightseeing
登高望远	climb atop to have a panoramic view
全家出游	family outing
去远足	have an excursion
被指定为老人节	be designated as the Senior's Festival
表达对长者的尊敬	express respect for elders
探访年长的亲戚	visit elderly relatives

B3. Speaking Activities

Role Play

There is a variety of traditional festivals in China, each with abundant cultural significance. A TV program with a large international viewership is making a featured show to introduce the different traditional festivals in China. As journalists of this show, you and your colleagues need to **interview at least 5 students** about the celebration of the traditional festivals in China. Your questions might include:

- What is your favorite traditional festival? Why?
- When is the festival celebrated in lunar calendar?
- What is the origin or legend of this festival?
- What are the traditions of this festival?
- What is the typical food for this festival?

After the interview, summarize the main festivals and their celebrations and broadcast to international viewers. You may refer to the words and expressions in Part B, but don't confine yourself to them.

Pair Work

The Chinese dragon plays an important part in Chinese festivals. The Dragon Boat Festival is almost purely a dragon-related festival, which has become an internationally popular event. At special festivals, especially the Dragon Boat Festival, dragon boat races play an important part. The ancient Chinese dragon or loong has totally different symbolic meanings from Western dragons. Now work in pairs to complete the following table with the information about the respective appearance, power, associations, legends or stories and idioms of the Chinese loong and the Western dragon. You may refer to B4 in Part B or search online for more information.

	Chinese Loong	Western Dragon
Appearance		
Power		
Association		
Legends or stories		
Idioms		

Brainstorming

In recent years, some scholars suggest using *Pinyin* when introducing Chinese cultural terms, such as using *jiaozi* for Chinese dumpling, or loong for the Chinese dragon. They believe that it is an effective way to boost Chinese cultural confidence. While others assert that it is not helpful to publicize and promote Chinese cultures overseas. What do you think of their ideas? What do you think is **the best way to introduce Chinese cultural terms**? Please elaborate on your views.

Read and Tell

Read the following paragraphs about **the dragon boat race** and tell the Chinese stories.

The dragon boat race was performed for the first time in the Tokyo 2020 Olympic Games, introducing ancient Chinese culture to the rest of the world. The ten-minute performance has been displayed between canoe races at the Sea Forest Waterway from August 2 to 7, kicking off the procedure of the dragon boat race entering the Olympic Games.

As a representative of Chinese culture, the dragon boat race is best known and long believed as a traditional practice of the Dragon Boat Festival to commemorate the patriotic poet Qu Yuan (340 B.C.-278 B.C.) during the Warring States period of ancient China.

The competitive dragon boat race is different from the traditional dragon boat race. Traditionally, there are three different paddling postures — paddlers can sit, kneel or stand on the boat. Since 2008, the International Dragon Boat Federation has stipulated paddlers to take the seat posture in all international dragon boat races. The drummer and the player of gong, a traditional Chinese musical instrument, are the soul of a traditional race team. But the competitive dragon boat race only keeps the drummer in the front of the boat. In terms of the number of participants, there can be as many as 36 people on a traditional dragon boat, while there are usually 12 or 22 people on a competitive dragon boat. And this time in the Tokyo Olympics, the number of participants is further reduced to 10 on a boat.

(Adapted from *CGTN.com*)

Ideas for Telling:

- Trace the origin and development of the dragon boat race.
- Discuss its new face at the Olympics.

Debate

An increasing number of Chinese are fond of celebrating Western festivals today. In comparison, traditional Chinese festivals as Spring Festival, the Festival of Lanterns and Mid-Autumn Festival seem to be losing their attraction. In view of such a situation, many are worried that Chinese culture will be ignored or even ruined by the invasion of Western festivals. Others believe that we needn't be over worried. Because the increasing popularity of some Western festivals in China is nothing accidental, but something justifiable.

(Adapted from *CHINADAILY.com.cn*)

Topic for Debate:

While we are giving priority to the preservation and development of traditional Chinese culture, we needn't worry too much about the inflow of foreign culture.

Interpretation

Use the words and expressions you learned from Part B of this unit to interpret the paragraphs below into English.

Paragraph 1

中秋节，又称月亮节、团圆节等，是中国民间的传统节日。对于中国人而言，中秋节的重要性仅次于春节。中秋节自古便有祭月、赏月、吃月饼、看花灯、赏桂花、饮桂花酒等民俗，流传至今，经久不息。其中，吃月饼已经是我国南北各地过中秋节的必备习俗。月饼象征着大团圆，作为一种节日食品，人们将它赠送亲友或用以祭月。

Paragraph 2

端午节与春节、清明节、中秋节并称为中国四大传统节日。传说战国时期的楚国诗人屈原，在五月初五跳汨罗江自尽，因此后人将端午节作为纪念屈原的节日。端午节的习俗包括吃粽子、赛龙舟等。端午文化在世界上影响广泛，不少国家和地区均有庆贺端午的活动。2006 年 5 月，国务院将其列入首批国家级非物质文化遗产名录；自 2008 年起，被列为国家法定节假日。2009 年 9 月，联合国教科文组织正式批准将其列入《人类非物质文化遗产代表作名录》,端午节成为中国首个入选世界非遗的节日。

Paragraph 3

重阳节,是中国民间传统节日,节期在每年农历九月初九。“九”在《易经》中为阳数,“九九”两阳数相重,故曰“重阳”。古人认为九九重阳是吉祥的日子。登高赏秋与感恩敬老是当今重阳节日活动的两大重要主题。重阳节在历史发展演变中杂糅多种民俗为一体,承载了丰富的文化内涵。在民俗观念中“九”在数字中是最大数,有长久长寿的含意,寄托着人们对老人健康长寿的祝福。2006 年 5 月 20 日,重阳节被国务院列入首批国家级非物质文化遗产名录。

B4. Culture Highlights

Q: *What are the differences between Chinese loong and Western dragon?*

A: Chinese loong and western dragon are two different creatures, both of them are virtual, and first created in mythologies and tales, and have roots in religion, then elaborated in literature works. Chinese loong is a noble divine creature, with the symbolic meanings of fortune, good luck, peace, authority and prosperity; while western dragon is belittled as an emblem of the evil, greedy for gold, with the symbolic meaning of destroy and deceiving.

Chinese loong is a large virtual snake-like creature whose body has a saying of Nine Resembles, which maybe is a method to underline its powers. It has sharp claws of eagle, hard scales of fish, agile neck of snake, and antlers of a deer, and its physical appearance varies according to different records. While western dragon is a large virtual lizard-like monster with scales, horns, bat-like wings, fours legs and a long tail.

As for their unique powers, Chinese loong lives in waters, controlling thunder, lightning and water, and summoning cloud, and it has the power of flying, like floating in the air, and swimming in waters; western dragon lives in underground lair, having the powers of breathing fire, and flying as it has leathery wings.

From the very beginning, the images of dragon in west countries and loong in Chinese culture are set, and they don't change in the several thousand years. Western dragon is more of a negative character, an outrageous monster, which makes the heroes valiant and renowned, who defeat and slay the evil dragon. While Chinese loong is famous for its strong power and kindness and benevolence, which helps god and human beings remove obstacles and overcome difficulties, and brings rains to dry crops harvest to farmers.

(Adapted from *topchinatravel.com*)

Q: *Each of the Chinese festivals features the eating of a particular food among their customs. Why?*

A: China is a country with a long history, and food has played an important role in the development of Chinese culture. Every year many traditional festivals and events are celebrated with special foods. Some of these foods have particular meanings, such as good luck, best wishes, unity, and commemoration.

Dating back at least 2,000 years, the symbolism of foods in China comes from superstitions or traditional beliefs in eating to invoke/celebrate blessing. A meaning or "power" is associated with foods through food name pronunciation, food shape, colors, food history/legends, and so on. For example, dumplings or *nian gao* eating during the Spring Festival, *zongzi* at Dragon Boat Festival, mooncakes at Mid-Autumn Festival and so on.

Besides festival foods, there are other foods with symbolic meanings eaten at special occasions to invoke (or celebrate) a specific blessing. For example, newly-married couples are supposed to eat seeds at weddings because *zi*, or seeds in mandarin is homophonous to fertility. Noodles and peaches are usually offered on birthday feasts because they symbolize longevity.

(Adapted from *Chinahighlights.com* & *BetterChinese.com*)

B5. Extension

Synonym Discrimination

Can you figure out the differences among the words and phrases below?

Group 1: worship / honour / pay tribute to / offer sacrifice to / pay respect to

Group 2: faithful / loyal / devoted / dedicated

Extensive Reading

The History and Traditions of Qixi Festival

The Qixi Festival, or Double Seventh Festival, is one of Chinese traditional festivals. It is also known as the Chinese Valentine's Day. It's based on a romantic legend about a weaver girl and an ox herd. According to legend, an oxherd, or Niulang, with the help of his ox (the demoted cattle god) married a fairy, Zhinü, who became a weaver girl. Zhinü's mother, a goddess, was angry and took Zhinü back to heaven. Niulang pursued using the ox's hide. The goddess separated them by a river of stars, the Milky Way, but magpies were allowed to form a bridge for them to meet once a year.

The festival has been celebrated since the Han Dynasty (206 BC-220 AD). On May 20, 2015, the Double Seventh Festival was added to the National Intangible Cultural Heritage list by the State Council of China. Many of the traditional customs are disappearing, or no longer observed. You are more likely to find these practiced in rural areas:

- Showing skills (demonstrating dexterity) was the most popular custom for women in the evening of Qixi. The longest standing way to "plead skills" was to speedily thread a needle under moonlight. Young women also carved exotic flowers, animals, and unusual birds, usually on a melon skin.
- Worshiping the weaver fairy (the star Vega) with a table of offerings: tea, wine, fruits, longans, red dates, hazelnuts, peanuts, and melon seeds. In the evening young women sat around the table, displaying their needlework, gazing at Vega, and praying for a good husband and a happy life. Then they'd play games or read poems until midnight.
- Honoring oxen: Children picked bunches of wild flowers and hung them on the horns of oxen in honor of the legendary ox.
- Eating "Skill Fruits" or *qiaoguo*, which are fried, thin pastries of different shapes.

Now people usually celebrate Chinese Valentine's Day by giving flowers, chocolates, and other presents to their sweethearts, instead of doing the traditional customs. Though in Chinese cities, Western Valentine's Day is now more popular than Qixi with young people, the romantic legend of Niulang and Zhinü has taken deep root in the hearts of Chinese people. It probably always will be told from one generation to the next.

(Adapted from *chinahighlights.com*)

Tomb-Sweeping Day in China

Tomb-Sweeping Day is a one-day Chinese holiday that has been celebrated in China for centuries. The day is meant to commemorate and pay respect to a person's ancestors. Thus, on Tomb-Sweeping Day, families visit and clean the gravesite of their ancestors to show their respect.

In addition to visiting cemeteries, people also go for walks in the countryside, plant willows, and fly kites. Those who cannot travel back to their ancestors' gravesites may opt to pay their respects at martyrs parks to pay homage to revolutionary martyrs.

Tomb-Sweeping Day

Tomb-Sweeping Day is held 107 days after the start of winter and is celebrated on April 4 or April 5, depending on the lunar calendar. Tomb-Sweeping Day is a national holiday in China with most people having the day off from work or school to allow time to travel to ancestral gravesites.

Origins

Tomb-Sweeping Day is based on the Hanshi Festival, which is also known as the Cold Food Festival and Smoke-Banning Festival. While the Hanshi Festival is no longer celebrated today, it has gradually been absorbed into Tomb-Sweeping Day festivities.

The Hanshi Festival commemorated Jie Zitui, a loyal court official from the Spring and Autumn Period. Jie was a loyal minister to Chong Er. During a civil war, Prince Chong Er and Jie fled and were in exile for 19 years. According to legend, Jie was so loyal during the exile that he even made broth out of the flesh of his leg to feed the prince when they were short of food. When Chong Er later became king, he rewarded those who helped him when times were tough; however, he overlooked Jie.

Many advised Jie to remind Chong Er that he, too, should be repaid for his loyalty. Instead, Jie packed his bags and relocated to the mountainside. When Chong Er discovered his oversight, he was ashamed. He went to look for Jie in the mountains. The conditions were harsh and he was unable to find Jie. Someone suggested that Chong Er set fire to the forest to force Jie out. After the king set fire to the forest, Jie didn't appear.

When the fire was extinguished, Jie was found dead with his mother on his back. He was under a willow tree and a letter written in blood was found in a hole in the tree. The letter read:

Giving meat and heart to my lord, hoping my lord will always be upright. An invisible ghost under a willow is better than a loyal minister beside my lord. If my lord has a place in his heart for me, please make self-reflection when remembering me. I have a clear consciousness in the nether world, being pure and bright in my offices year after year.

To commemorate Jie's death, Chong Er created the Hanshi Festival and ordered that no fire could be set on this day. Meaning, only cold food could be eaten. One year later, Chong Er went back to the willow tree to hold a memorial ceremony and found the willow tree in bloom again. The willow was named "Pure Bright White" and the Hanshi Festival became known as "Pure Brightness Festival". Pure Brightness is a fitting name for the festival because the weather is usually bright and clear in early April.

How Tomb-Sweeping Day is celebrated

Tomb-Sweeping Day is celebrated with families reuniting and traveling to their ancestors' gravesites to pay their respects. First, weeds are removed from the gravesite and the tombstone is cleaned and swept. Any necessary repairs to the gravesite are also made. The new earth is added and willow branches are placed atop the gravesite.

Next, joss sticks are placed by the grave. The sticks are then lit and an offering of food and paper money is placed at the tomb. Paper money is burned while family members show their respect by bowing to their ancestors. Fresh flowers are placed at the tomb and some families also plant willow trees. In ancient times, the five-colored paper was placed underneath a stone on the grave to signify that someone had visited the grave and that it had not been abandoned.

As cremation is gaining popularity, families continue the tradition by making offerings at ancestral altars or by placing wreaths and flowers at martyrs' shrines. Due to hectic work schedules and the long-distance, some families must travel, some families opt to mark the festival earlier or later in April over a long weekend or assign a few family members to make the trip on behalf of the entire family.

Once the family has paid their respects at the gravesite, some families will have a picnic at the gravesite. Then, they take advantage of the usually good weather to take a walk in the countryside, known as *taqing*, hence another name for the festival, Taqing Festival.

Some people wear a willow twig on their heads to keep ghosts away. Another custom includes picking shepherd's purse flower. Women also pick herbs and make dumplings with them and they also wear the shepherd's purse flower in their hair.

Other traditional activities on Tomb-Sweeping Day include playing tug-of-war and swinging on swings. It is also a good time for sowing and other agricultural activities, including planting willow trees.

(Adapted from *thoughtco.com*)

B6. Assignment

Poster Design

Form **groups of 3 or 4** and **design an English poster** featuring the Mid-Autumn Festival. You need to:

- Discuss what festival elements or words should be included.
- Design the layout of the festival elements and words.

- Print and share the poster with your classmates.
- Explain the design process on class.

References

The Lunar New Year: Rituals and Legends. *Asia for Educators*. Retrieved from http://afe.easia.columbia.edu/special/china_general_lunar.htm on March 15, 2022.

Chinese New Year. *Wikipedia*. Retrieved from https://en.wikipedia.org/wiki/Chinese_New_Year on March 15, 2022.

Chinese Spring Festival. *Top China Travel*. Retrieved from https://www.topchinatravel.com/china-guide/spring-festival.htm on March 15, 2022.

Monica Bhide. How Eating Whole Fish Could Bring Good Luck. *Cooking Channel*. Retrieved from https://www.cookingchanneltv.com/devour/2013/06/how-eating-whole-fish-could-bring-good-luck on March 15, 2022.

Lantern Festival: The "Real" Chinese Valentine's Day. *Beijing Tourism*. Retrieved from https://english.visitbeijing.com.cn/article/47OO1ZSqm0d on March 15, 2022.

Fercility Jiang. The Differences Between the Chinese Zodiac and Western Astrology. *China Highlights*. Retrieved from https://www.chinahighlights.com/travelguide/chinese-zodiac/chinese-vs-western-astrology.htm on March 15, 2022.

Chinese New Year Firecrackers: Why Set Off and Meaning. *China Highlights*. Retrieved from https://www.chinahighlights.com/travelguide/festivals/chinese-new-year-firecrackers.htm on March 15, 2022

The Story of Dragon Boat Festival. *China Culture*. Retrieved from http://en.chinaculture.org/focus/focus/2010duanwu/2010-06/13/content_382651.htm on March 15, 2022.

Fercility Jiang. 7 Facts to Learn Chinese Dragon Boat Festival. *China Highlights*. Retrieved from https://www.chinahighlights.com/festivals/dragon-boat-festival-fact.htm on March 15, 2022.

The Dragon Boat Festival. UNESCO. Retrieved from https://www.unesco.org/archives/multimedia/document-335 on March 15, 2022.

Fercility Jiang. Mid-Autumn Festival (Mooncake Festival): Celebrations, Greetings, Origins. *China Highlights*. Retrieved from https://www.chinahighlights.com/festivals/mid-autumn-festival.htm on March 15, 2022.

Muhammad Asim Raza. Growing Popularity of Western Festivals in China No Cause for

Alarm. *China Daily*. Retrieved from http://www.chinadaily.com.cn/opinion/2015-12/29/content_22855326.htm on March 15, 2022.

Chinese Dragon VS Western Dragon. *Top China Travel*. Retrieved from https://www.topchinatravel. com/china-guide/chinese-dragon-and-western-dragon. htm on March 15, 2022.

Tracing Origin of Dragon Boat Race, a New Face at the Olympics. *CGTN*. Retrieved from https://news. cgtn. com/news/2021-08-05/Tracing-origin-of-dragon-boat-race-a-new-face-at-the-Olympics-12u8RPaODjq/index.html on March 15, 2022.

Fercility Jiang. Qixi Festival — How to Celebrate Chinese Valentine's Day. *China Highlights*. Retrieved from https://www.chinahighlights.com/festivals/double-seventh-festival.htm on March 15, 2022.

Lauren Mack. Tomb-Sweeping Day in China. *Thoughtco*. Retrieved from https://www.thoughtco.com/tomb-sweeping-festival-687518 on March 15, 2022.

Unit 2 Chinese Life Course

Part A Life Stages

A1. Introduction

The Twelve Stages of the Human Life Cycle

Which stage of life is the most important? Some might claim that infancy is the key stage, when a baby's brain is wide open to new experiences that will influence all the rest of its later life. Others might argue that it's adolescence or young adulthood when physical health is at its peak. Many cultures around the world value late adulthood more than any other, arguing that it is at this stage that the human being has finally acquired the wisdom necessary to guide others. Who is right? The truth of the matter is that every stage of life is equally significant and necessary for the welfare of humanity. In my book *The Human Odyssey: Navigating the Twelve Stages of Life*, I've written that each stage of life has its own unique "gift" to contribute to the world. We need to value each one of these gifts if we are to truly support the deepest needs of human life. Here are what I call the twelve gifts of the human life cycle:

- **Pre-birth: Potential** — The child who has not yet been born could become anything — a Michelangelo, a Shakespeare, a Martin Luther King — and thus holds for all of humanity the principle of what we all may yet become in our lives.
- **Birth: Hope** — When a child is born, it instills in its parents and other caregivers a sense of optimism; a sense that this new life may bring something new and special into the world. Hence, the newborn represents the sense of hope that we all nourish inside of ourselves to make the world a better place.
- **Infancy (Ages 0-3): Vitality** — The infant is a vibrant and seemingly unlimited

source of energy. Babies thus represent the inner dynamo of humanity, ever fueling the fires of the human life cycle with new channels of psychic power.

- **Early Childhood (Ages 4-6): Playfulness** — When young children play, they recreate the world anew. They take what is and combine it with what is possible to fashion events that have never been seen before in the history of the world. As such, they embody the principle of innovation and transformation that underlies every single creative act that has occurred during civilization.
- **Middle Childhood (Ages 7-8): Imagination** — In middle childhood, the sense of an inner subjective self develops for the first time, and this self is alive with images taken in from the outer world and brought up from the depths of the unconscious. This imagination serves as a source of creative inspiration in later life for artists, writers, scientists, and anyone else who finds their days and nights enriched for having nurtured a deep inner life.
- **Late Childhood (Ages 9-11): Ingenuity** — Older children have acquired a wide range of social and technical skills that enable them to come up with marvelous strategies and inventive solutions for dealing with the increasing pressures that society places on them. This principle of ingenuity lives on in that part of ourselves that ever seeks new ways to solve practical problems and cope with everyday responsibilities.
- **Adolescence (Ages 12-20): Passion** — The biological event of puberty unleashes a powerful set of changes in the adolescent body that reflect themselves in a teenager's sexual, emotional, cultural, and / or spiritual passion. Adolescence passion thus represents a significant touchstone for anyone who is seeking to reconnect with their deepest inner zeal for life.
- **Early Adulthood (Ages 21-35): Enterprise** — It takes enterprise for young adults to accomplish their many responsibilities, including finding a home and mate, establishing a family or circle of friends, and / or getting a good job. This principle of enterprise thus serves us at any stage of life when we need to go out into the world and make our mark.
- **Midlife (Ages 36-50): Contemplation** — After many years in young adulthood of following society's scripts for creating a life, people in midlife often take a break from worldly responsibilities to reflect upon the deeper meaning of their lives, the better to forge ahead with new understanding. This element of contemplation represents an important resource that we can all draw upon to deepen and enrich our lives at any age.
- **Mature Adulthood (Ages 51-80): Benevolence** — Those in mature adulthood have raised families, established themselves in their work life, and become

contributors to the betterment of society through volunteerism, mentorships, and other forms of philanthropy. All of the humanity benefits from their benevolence. Moreover, we all can learn from their examples to give more of ourselves to others.

- **Late Adulthood (Age 80+): Wisdom** — Those with long lives have acquired a rich repository of experiences that they can use to help guide others. Elders thus represent the source of wisdom that exists in each of us, helping us to avoid the mistakes of the past while reaping the benefits of life's lessons.
- **Death & Dying: Life** — Those in our lives who are dying, or who have died, teach us about the value of living. They remind us not to take our lives for granted, but to live each moment of life to its fullest, and to remember that our own small lives form a part of a greater whole.

Since each stage of life has its own unique gift to give to humanity, we need to do whatever we can to support each stage and protect each stage from attempts to suppress its individual contribution to the human life cycle. Thus, we need to be wary, for example, of attempts to thwart a young child's need to play through the establishment of high-pressure formal academic preschools. We should protect the wisdom of the aged from elder abuse. We need to do what we can to help our adolescents at risk. We need to advocate for prenatal education and services for poor mothers and support safe and healthy birthing methods in third world countries. We ought to take the same attitude toward nurturing the human life cycle as we do toward saving the environment from global warming and industrial pollutants. For by supporting each stage of the human life cycle, we will help to ensure that all its members are given care and helped to blossom to their fullest degree.

(Adapted from *institute4learning.com*)

A2. Words and Expressions

Vocabulary

1. infant /ˈɪnfənt/ *n*. 婴儿
2. toddler /ˈtɒdlər/ *n*. (尤指处于学步期或刚学会走路的)幼童
3. adolescent /ˌædəˈlesənt/ *n*. 青少年
4. threshold /ˈθreʃhəʊld/ *n*. 门槛;阈,界限;起点
5. compulsory /kəmˈpʌlsəri/ *adj*. 必须做的;强制性的;必修的
6. tertiary /ˈtɜːʃəri/ *adj*. 第三的;第三级的;高等教育的,大学教育的
7. vocational /vəʊˈkeɪʃənəl/ *adj*. 职业的;业务的

生命阶段	Life Stages
婴幼儿(0—1 岁)	infant / baby
婴幼儿期	infancy
学步儿童(1—3 岁)	toddler
学步期	toddlerhood
学前儿童(3—5 岁)	preschooler
儿童,孩子(2—12 岁)	child
童年,幼年时代	childhood
幼儿期	early childhood
学龄儿童(6—12 岁)	school children
童年中期	middle childhood
十至十二岁的少年	tween / tweenager
青春期前期	preadolescence
青少年(13—18 岁)	adolescent
青春期	adolescence
十几岁的少年(13—19 岁)	teenager
刚成年的年轻人(18—24 岁)	thresholder / young adult
二十来岁(20—29 岁)	twentysomething
青年	youth
而立之年	thirties
三十多岁(30—39 岁)	in one's thirties
中年人(40—60 岁)	the middle-aged
中年	middle age
中年发福	middle-age spread
老年人(60 岁以上)	the elderly
老年	old age

教育阶段	Education Stages
托儿所	child care center
幼儿园	kindergarten
学前班	preschool
义务教育	compulsory education
小学教育	primary education
小学	primary school
中学教育	secondary education
初中	junior (lower) secondary school
中考	senior high school entrance examination
高中	senior (upper) secondary school

高考	National College Entrance Examination (NCEE)
职业教育	vocational education
中专	vocational senior secondary school
高等教育	tertiary education
学士学位	Bachelor's degree
硕士学位	Master's degree
博士学位(最高学位)	Doctor's degree / Ph.D. (Doctor of Philosophy)
博士后(研究经历)	postdoctor

Vocabulary

1. oosperm /ˈəʊəˌspɜːm/ *n.* 受精卵
2. fetal /ˈfiːt(ə)l/ *adj.* 胎儿的
3. embryo /ˈembriəʊ/ *n.* 胚,胚胎
4. eutocia /jʊˈtəʊʃɪə/ *n.* 正常分娩;顺产
5. confinement /kənˈfaɪnmənt/ *n.* 分娩,生产
6. patchwork /ˈpætʃwɜːk/ *n.* 拼布工艺(品)
7. zodiac /ˈzəʊdiæk/ *n.* 黄道带(指太阳、月亮和行星组成的假想带,分成十二个等份区,各有其名称和符号,并和一年中特定的时间相关);黄道十二宫图

出生	Birth
受精卵	oosperm
怀孕	pregnancy
胚胎	embryo
产房;分娩室	delivery room
生孩子	give birth (to)
接生	deliver
顺产	natural labor / eutocia
剖宫产	C-section
无痛分娩	painless labor / painless delivery
坐月子	30-day confinement period
三朝礼	Three Days Celebration / San Zhao Li
三朝洗儿	bath the baby in the Three Days Celebration
满月礼	Full Month Celebration / Man Yue Li
满月宴	Full Month Banquet

百日礼	A Hundred Days Celebration / Bai Ri Li
百家衣	Patchwork Clothes / Bai Jia Yi
长命锁	Longevity Lock / Chang Ming Suo
剃胎发	shave fetal hair
生肖,属相	Chinese zodiac signs

Vocabulary

1. abacus /'æbəkəs/ *n*. 算盘
2. enlightenment /ɪn'laɪtənmənt/ *n*. 领悟;启发;开导
3. prevail /prɪ'veɪl/ *v*. 占优势,占上风;流行,盛行
4. seal /siːl/ *n*. 封蜡;印章;封条
5. studious /'stjuːdiəs/ *adj*. 好学的;勤奋的,用功的
6. excel /ɪk'sel/ *v*. 擅长,善于;突出

周岁礼	**One-Year-Old Celebration**
抓周	Draw Lots / One-Year-Old Catch
盛行	prevail in
追溯到	trace back to
重要的传统习俗	important traditional customs
庆祝第一个生日	celebrate the first birthday
放置象征性物品	place symbolic items
从物品中选择	choose from the articles
预测未来	predict the future
预测兴趣和职业	foretell interests and career
表达美好祝愿	express good wishes
进行启蒙教育	conduct enlightenment education
抓了钱意味着发大财	reaching for money could make a fortune
抓了书意味着爱读书	reaching for books could like reading
抓了印章意味着会当官	reaching for a seal could become an official
抓了文具意味着好学	reaching for school supplies could be studious
抓了算盘意味着善于理财	reaching for abacus could be good at financing
抓了吃食意味着有口福	reaching for food could eat well
抓了炊事用具意味着善于烹饪	reaching for cooker could excel in cooking

Vocabulary

1. pin /pɪn/ *n.* (尤指用于固定布料用的)别针,大头针;饰针;胸针
2. bun /bʌn/ *n.* 圆发髻
3. divination /ˌdɪvɪˈneɪʃən/ *n.* 占卜,算命
4. coil /kɔɪl/ *n.* (绳索、头发或电线的)卷,圈,盘
5. knot /nɒt/ *n.* 绞成一团的头发(或绳)
6. dignity /ˈdɪgnəti/ *n.* 庄重,端庄;尊严
7. kowtow /ˌkaʊˈtaʊ/ *v.* 卑躬屈膝,唯命是从
8. courtesy /ˈkɜːtəsi/ *n.* 谦恭有礼的举止,礼貌;礼节;客气话
9. honorific /ˌɒnərˈɪfɪk/ *adj.* 表示尊敬的
10. clan /klæn/ *n.* 家族,氏族;(享有共同利益的)群体,集团

成人礼	**Coming-of-age Ceremony**
冠礼(古时男子满 20 岁)	capping ceremony
笄礼(古时女子满 15 岁)	hair-pinning ceremony
卜日(通过占卜选择日期)	choose date by divination
正宾	the honored guest
加冠	do the hair up in a bun or coil and wear a cap
加笄	gather hair into a knot and use a hairpin to hold it in place
致贺词	deliver a congratulatory speech
像成年人一样行事	act as an adult
维护尊严	maintain dignity
践行高尚品德	achieve moral excellence
聆训	listen to his / her parents' teaching or expectation
向父母磕头	kowtow to parents
字冠者(笄者)	give a Courtesy Name or honorific name
向所有来宾鞠躬致谢	bow and show gratitude to all the guests for attending
标志着步入成年	signal the entry into adulthood
可以结婚	be qualified to get married
继承权力和头衔	inherit power and titles
承担成人责任	take adult responsibilities
参加社会活动	participate in social activities
被氏族和社会所接受	be accepted by the clan and society

Vocabulary

1. grand /grænd/ *adj*. 重大的;主要的;首要的
2. kindle /ˈkɪndəl/ *v*. 点燃
3. jubilant /ˈdʒuːbələnt/ *adj*. (尤指因成功而)欢欣的,喜气洋洋的
4. longevity /lɒnˈdʒevəti/ *n*. 长寿
5. confectionery /kənˈfekʃənri/ *n*. 甜食;糖果;巧克力
6. wheaten /ˈwiːtən/ *adj*. 小麦的;小麦制成的
7. etiquette /ˈetɪket/ *n*. 礼仪,礼节;规范,规矩
8. filial piety /ˈfɪliəl ˈpaɪəti/ 孝顺;孝心

过寿	**Celebrate Birthday for the Elderly**
花甲	a cycle of sixty years
古稀	seventy years of age
耄耋	old age
年过花甲	over one's sixtieth
年近古稀	approach seventy years of age
儿孙满堂	have a big family filled with children and grandchildren
盛大的庆典	a grand celebration
邀请亲朋好友	invite relatives and friends
营造欢乐的气氛	kindle a jubilant atmosphere
表示感谢	show appreciation
赠送礼物	give presents
具有象征意义的食物	foods with symbolic implications
长寿面	long-life / longevity noodles
不被剪断	not to be cut short
寿桃	longevity peach(fresh or confectionery peaches offered as a birthday gift)
甜馅蒸面食	steamed wheaten food with sweet fillings
做成桃子的形状	be made in the shape of peaches
献桃贺寿	celebrate birthday with peaches
象征长寿	symbolize a long life / longevity
孝敬的文化礼仪	the cultural etiquette of filial piety
向……致以最美好的祝愿	extend one's best wishes to...

福如东海，寿比南山。	Happiness is like the East China Sea and longevity is better than the south mountain.

Vocabulary

1. obituary /ə'bɪtʃʊəri/ *n*. (尤指报纸上的)讣告，讣闻
2. vigil /'vɪdʒəl/ *n*. (陪伴病人、祈祷、表达不同政见等的)不眠时间；(尤指)值夜，守夜
3. somber /'sɑːmbə/ *adj*. 严肃的；忧郁的；暗淡的，深色的
4. condolence /kən'dəʊləns/ *n*. 吊唁(词)；哀悼(词)
5. corpse /kɔːps/ *n*. (通常指人的)尸体
6. incense /'ɪnsens/ *n*. (尤指在宗教仪式上焚烧的)香
7. cremation /krə'meɪʃn/ *n*. 火葬，火化
8. urn /ɜːn/*n*. 瓮；骨灰瓮
9. inhumation /ˌɪnhjuː'meɪʃn/ *n*. 土葬，埋葬

死亡	**Death**
死者	the deceased (person)
讣告	obituary
儒家的孝道	the Confucian principle of filial piety
穿深色衣服	wear somber clothes
微微鞠躬	give a slight bow
服丧戴的黑纱	mourning band
丧服	mourning clothes
吊唁；哀悼	condolence
花圈	wreaths
棺材	coffin
灵柩	a coffin containing a corpse
守灵	wake
通宵守夜	keep all-night vigils
葬礼	funeral
埋葬；安葬	bury
火葬	cremation
火葬，火化	cremate
骨灰盒	cremation urn

公墓,墓地	cemetery
祠堂	ancestral hall
灵牌	ancestral tablet
香(祭祀专用)	joss stick
焚香点烛	burn incense and light candles
纸钱	paper money (paper made to resemble money and burned as an offering to the dead)
烧纸	burn paper money
辟邪	ward off evil spirits
为死者带来安宁	bring peace to the deceased
保佑后代	protect their descendants

Vocabulary

1. tribute /ˈtrɪbjuːt/ *n*. (尤指在正式场合表达敬意的)颂词,礼物
2. insert /ɪnˈsɜːt/ *v*. 插入;添加(文字、表格等)
3. verdant /ˈvɜːdənt/ *adj*. 长满绿色植物的;草木苍翠的
4. chrysanthemum /krɪˈsænθəməm/ *n*. 菊花
5. descendant /dɪˈsendənt/ *n*. 子孙,后代
6. venerate /ˌvenəˈreɪt/ *v*. 尊重;敬重
7. reverence /ˈrevərəns/ *n*. 尊敬;崇敬
8. nostalgia /nɒsˈtældʒə/ *n*. 对往事的怀念,怀旧,念旧
9. shrine /ʃraɪn/ *n*. 圣地;神龛;圣坛;神殿

祭祖	**Ancestor Worship**
除夕祭祖	New Year's Eve ancestor worship
重阳节	Chung Yeung / Double Ninth Festival
重阳祭祖	Chung Yeung ancestor worship
中元节	Zhongyuan/ Hungry Ghost Festival
中元祭祖	Zhongyuan ancestor worship
清明节	Qingming / Tomb-Sweeping Festival
清明祭祖	Qingming ancestor worship
寒食节	Cold Food Festival
吃青团	eat sweet green rice balls
供贡品	offer tribute

放鞭炮	light firecrackers
磕头祭祖	worship ancestors with kowtows
表示尊敬之意	show reverence
表达怀念之情	express nostalgia
安抚祖先灵魂	pacify the spirits of the ancestors
保佑子孙后代	bless for future generations
为后代带来好运	bring luck to descendants
扫墓	sweep tomb
赞扬,称赞	pay tribute to...
去墓地	make a visit to the gravesite
送鲜花	present fresh flowers
菊花和百合	chrysanthemums and lilies
纪念死者	commemorate the deceased
祭奠先人	venerate the forebears
祈求保护	pray for their protection
提供祭祀食物	offer sacrificial food
用新的土壤覆盖坟墓	cover the tomb with new soil
在坟墓上插入青翠的树枝	insert verdant branches on the tomb
为祖先保留牌位或神龛	keep tablets or shrines for ancestors

A3. Speaking Activities

Situational Speech

Imagine that you are an undergraduate student, and you are sharing **Chinese Ancestor Worship Culture** with international students. Prepare a 5-minute speech. Your speech might cover:

- The days or the festivals to conduct ancestor worship.
- Customs and activities about ancestor worship.
- The significance of the Chinese ancestor worship to people.

You may refer to the words and expressions in Part A, but please don't confine yourself to them.

Brainstorm

From birth to death, there are so many stages we should experience in our whole life time, **such as toddler, childhood, adolescence, youth, middle-age, old age...** when it comes to the stages you have experienced, share your viewpoints on the following topics.

- Which stage is the most important one? Why?
- Which stage is the most unforgettable one? Why?
- Which stage is the happiest one? Why?
- If you could live your life all over again, which stage do you like to go back to and what would you do differently?

Read and Share

Read the following paragraphs about National College Entrance Examination (NCEE) in China and share your views.

The NCEE, also named gaokao in China, is an examination that is taken by Chinese students in their last year of high school typically from June 7 to June 8 or 9. It is also the lone criterion for admission into Chinese universities. One Chinese saying aptly compares the exam to a stampede of "thousands of soldiers and tens of thousands of horses across a single log bridge."

Though varying from province to province, the gaokao generally includes tests of Chinese literature, mathematics and a foreign language (in most cases English). If students choose liberal arts as specialty in high school, they need to take additional tests related to history, politics and geography. If they choose science, they'll take physics, chemistry and biology tests.

The higher the gaokao score is, the more likely a student will gain admittance into the prestigious universities in China. As you can imagine, the preparation for such a high-stake and make-or-break exam is a long and grueling process, when students do practice exams almost every day while books and exam papers can be seen piled up high on their desks. Many students have spent the last 2-3 years specifically preparing for this exam.

(Adapted from *thatsmags.com*)

Ideas for Sharing:

- What is the significance of gaokao to your life?
- Take gaokao as your milestone in your life, what do you think your next milestone will be? How are you going to cross it?
- Is our life full of "gaokaos"? Why? How can we face each one in our lifetime with ease?

Discussion

Fate vs. Destiny

Fate and destiny both can be translated into "命运" in Chinese, but the deep meaning of them is quite different. Fate is something beyond your control. You can't change your fate. Fate can be cruel. Fighting your fate is an impossible battle. Sometimes, it's hard to accept your fate, like your family background, your gene, your character, etc.

While destiny can be shaped by your choices. Destiny is your future. Your actions determine the shape of your destiny. Each person's destiny is his own to make. You can be the master of your own destiny, like how much time you are going to spend on your study.

Topic to discuss: **Do you think your "命运" is fate or destiny? Why?** What can we do to change our destiny?

Interpretation

Use the words and expressions you learned from Part A of this unit to interpret the paragraphs below into English.

Paragraph 1

有人说:"人生有三个阶段,生存、生活、生命。"不管是生存阶段、生活阶段还是生命阶段,这与我们财富的多少、出身的贵贱甚至是文化程度的高低没有本质的联系,真正起决定作用的是我们的志向。不管是生存、生活还是生命,它们并不是相互独立和割裂的,而更多的是内心的追求和境界层次。有的人虽然家财万贯,可是汲汲一生却依然只停留在了生存的阶段。有的人虽然看着清贫,却早已到了了不得的境界。比如颜回,"一瓢饮,一箪食,在陋巷。人也不堪其忧,回也不改其乐。"不管其他走到了哪一个阶段,真正重要的是回归我们自身。

Paragraph 2

在老人过寿之时,身边的子女、亲朋便要进行一年一度的生日庆祝活动,俗称"祝寿"。为老人祝寿,要备制礼品,一般多以老人喜爱的食品、衣物为主。食品是面条和寿桃,生日蛋糕不可缺少,生日蛋糕的造型极具传统民俗特色,有寿桃型、寿星型的,上面还带有"福如东海""寿比南山"等字样。比较讲究的人家,也有撰写"寿联"和设"寿中堂"的。在老人生日当天,子女或亲友携带寿糕及食品等给老人祝寿,晚辈及亲友向老人敬酒、祝辞。

Paragraph 3

抓周是很多地方都会有的习俗。在宝宝周岁时,父母会将书、笔、算盘、刀剑等放在孩子面前让其任意选取,宝宝抓取不同的物品,寓意长大后将从事相关的职业。在宝宝周岁那天,父母要提前为宝宝梳洗干净,穿上新的衣服帽子,然后带宝宝祭拜祖先。之后布置抓周物品,选择宽敞的地方让宝宝开始抓取,家长同时也可以用相机将这个具有纪念意义的过程记录下来。

A4. Culture Highlights

Q: *What is the fortune telling in China?*

A: Many fortune tellers purely use ancient methods, supposedly containing ancient wisdom (though none of their predictions have been scientifically validated). Others compliment their methods with deductions based on your reactions, appearance, etc. for sometimes startling accuracy. In any case, prices are usually lower than in the West. One of the benefits of fortune telling for some is its entertainment value, like the thrill of live magic, or experiencing a real-life Sherlock Holmes try to read a person (you) at first sight.

If the soothsayer is good, you may well hear a few home truths (that are deducible by a perceptive person). A visit to a fortune teller might be as valuable as a visit to a psychologist or doctor or religious advisor!

The most common methods of Chinese fortune telling you will find throughout China are:

- Facial fortune telling: Telling your fortune using your facial features, or miànxiàng, use specific facial features associated with areas of your personality.
- Palmistry: Shǒuxiàng, or using the palm of one's hand to predict one's destiny, analyze the positioning of palm lines for love, personality, and other traits of your future. Chinese palmistry closely resembles Western palmistry in technique, using the seven major lines found on palms to gather the most important information about one's future.
- Horoscopy: Another method is known as Bāzì, which uses your natal data to tell your future. This method is based on the four pillars of destiny (birth year, birth month, birth date and birth hour), and the relationship between the five elements (wood, fire, earth, metal and water). In a nutshell, Bāzì uses your natal data and matches it to a matrix of metaphysical knowledge. Compared to Western astrology, which is based on the planets and stars, Bāzì is more calendar-based, though it still refers to the solar system.
- Fortune sticks: This final popular way to have your fortune told is one that you're likely to come across at Taoist temples. Qiúqiān employs a bundle of sticks with different Chinese characters inscribed on them (32, 60, or 100 sticks). You shake the cylinder until a stick drops out with a Chinese character inscribed in it. This character and its meanings are then used to predict your future. This method most resembles drawing lots, a lottery/raffle, tarot cards ...or fortune cookies, etc.

This method particularly will require you to bring someone who speaks Chinese, as the explanations and predictions are long-winded and rooted in traditional Chinese.

(Adapted from *www.chinahighlights.com*)

Q: *Why is paper money burned at Chinese funerals? Why do Chinese wear white at funerals?*

A: Burying grave goods and giving food offerings have always been part of the Chinese funeral ritual, and this has evolved into the practice of burning Joss paper at Chinese funerals. Sometimes called ghost money or spirit money, it is believed that the souls will need money in the realm of Diyu, where they are judged by Yan Wang, Lord of the Earthly Court, before being taken to heaven or hell.

The color white is associated with death in China, as in many Asian cultures. Sometimes a white banner is hung above the door of the bereaved household, and mourners often wear subdued colors. If the person who died was over 80 years, guests may wear shades of pink to the funeral ceremony as it is considered a longevity milestone, and people are encouraged to celebrate rather than mourn. The color red is never worn for funerals, as it symbolizes happiness and good fortune in Chinese culture (which is why it is the traditional color of Chinese New Year and Chinese weddings).

(Adapted from *funeralguide.co.uk*)

A5. Extension

Synonym Discrimination

Can you figure out the differences among the words and phrases below?

Group 1: longevity / lifespan / life expectancy
Group 2: make a will / make a wish
Group 3: burial / funeral

Extensive Reading

Passage One

Chinese Birth Rituals

For the Chinese, the family is regarded as the primary unit of society. A birth within the family therefore holds special significance for the community and is associated with a number of rituals. Although traditional birth observances have largely given way to practical concerns, the importance of this event continues to be marked by the practice of simplified rituals.

Pre-natal birth rituals

Chinese pre-natal birth observances involve both rituals of avoidance and protection so as to ensure the security of the mother and unborn child. Many rituals of avoidance are associated with the belief that the position of the fetus should not be disturbed in any way, and that failure to do so might result in a difficult birth, miscarriage, or injury to the child. Expectant mothers are, therefore, strongly discouraged from moving furniture or renovating the house during their pregnancy. In addition, they are urged to avoid activities such as digging, slaughtering, hammering, and looking at unsightly images as these would lead to undesirable consequences. Expectant mothers should also refrain from uttering words that are considered taboo or offensive to deities and spirits.

Chinese mothers also abstain from certain types of food during their pregnancy that are believed to be harmful to the baby. For example, pregnant Cantonese women are warned against consuming mutton, as the Cantonese word for meat has the same pronunciation as the word for epilepsy. On the other hand, Hokkien mothers are advised to avoid crabs as it is believed that doing so will result in the birth of a naughty child — literally born with as many "hands" as a crab. "Cooling" foods, which are associated with the reduction of heat or vitality, are also avoided as they may weaken the womb. At the same time, it is believed that certain foods should be taken to help strengthen the womb and ensure a smooth delivery. To give the child a smooth and fair complexion, expected mothers are recommended to take gingko fruits and strips of dried soya paste.

Post-natal birth rituals

The birth of a baby is usually followed by three customary rituals: confinement of the mother for a period of 30 days, ensuring that she is fed an appropriate and nutritious confinement diet, and making offerings to ancestors and deities.

Upon the birth of the baby, the mother is expected to remain at home during the *zuoyuezi* (坐月子) or "30-day confinement period". Complete rest facilitates her recuperation and she is encouraged to consume certain foods, in particular a dish of braised pig's trotters with ginger and vinegar. These supposedly help the mother regain her strength, regulate her body temperature and dispel air from the womb.

Today, Chinese families continue to observe all the three birth rituals to a limited extent. The demands of contemporary life, such as more women entering the workforce, the breakdown of the extended family system and the high expense of domestic help, have made it increasingly difficult for mothers to strictly practice these rituals.

First month celebrations

The Chinese regard the completion of the full 30 days since birth as the first birthday of the child or its "full moon". While the practice of rituals and scale of celebration may vary, most families still celebrate the 30th day or *manyue* (满月) of the baby's birth.

As *manyue* marks the beginning of the child's life in the community, his impending good health, happiness and success are paramount concerns of the celebrations. The belief is that these goals are attainable only if the appropriate words are spoken, the right behavior exemplified, and the necessary ritual symbols used.

This milestone also marks the time that the mother is allowed to take her first bath and wash her hair, while the ritual of hair shaving is also performed on the baby on this day. In some families, the baby would be dressed in new clothes, preferably red, as well as adorned with gold accessories to be presented to ancestors and deities at home. This is to inform the ancestors of the new addition to the household and to appeal to the spirits to protect the newborn.

The baby is also shown to relatives and friends for the first time during *manyue*. To indicate the completion of the child's "full moon", relatives and friends are presented with gifts. The types of gifts vary according to dialect group, and range from hard-boiled eggs, cakes and chicken to pickled ginger, savory glutinous rice and pig's trotters. The eggs, which have been dyed red for good luck, are an indispensable item as they symbolize the renewal of life. The shape of the egg is also associated with harmony and unity. Recipients are in turn expected to present the baby with gifts, usually gold jewelry or cash placed within *hongbao* or red packets. Some families choose to hold the *manyue* celebrations in a restaurant in the form of a dinner. The restaurant will prepare the red eggs and pickled ginger for guests.

(Adapted from *eresources.nlb.gov.sg*)

Passage Two

Chinese Funeral Traditions

Lauren Mack

While Chinese funeral traditions vary depending on where the deceased person and his or her family are from, some basic traditions still apply.

Funeral preparation

The job of coordinating and preparing Chinese funerals falls on the children or younger family members of the deceased person. It is part of the Confucian principle of filial piety and devotion to one's parents. Family members must consult the Chinese Almanac to determine the best date to hold the Chinese funeral ceremony. Funeral homes and local temples help the family prepare the body and coordinate the funeral rites.

Announcements of the funeral are sent in the form of invitations. For most Chinese funerals, the invitations are white. If the person was age 80 or older, then the invitations are pink. Living until 80 or beyond is considered a feat worth celebrating and mourners should celebrate the person's longevity rather than mourn.

The invitation includes information about the funeral's date, time, and location, as well as a small obituary that includes information about the deceased that may include his or her birth date, date of death, age, family members that survived them and sometimes how the person died. The invitation may also include a family tree.

A phone call or in-person invitation may precede the paper invitation. Either way, an RSVP is expected. If a guest cannot attend the funeral, the tradition is that he or she sends flowers and a white envelope with money.

Chinese funeral attire

Guests at a Chinese funeral wear somber colors like black. Bright and colorful clothing, especially red, must be avoided as these colors are associated with happiness. White is acceptable and, if the deceased was 80 or above, white with pink or red is acceptable as the event is cause for celebration. The deceased person wears a white robe.

The wake

There is often a wake preceding the funeral that may last several days. Family members are expected to keep an overnight vigil for at least one night in which the person's picture, flowers, and candles are placed on the body and the family sits near by.

During the wake, family and friends bring flowers, which are elaborate wreaths that include banners with couplets written on them, and white envelopes filled with cash. Traditional Chinese funeral flowers are white.

The white envelopes are similar to red envelopes that are given at weddings. White is the color reserved for death in Chinese culture. The amount of money put in the envelope varies depending on the relationship to the deceased but must be in odd numbers. The money is meant to help the family pay for the funeral. If the deceased person was employed, his or her company is often expected to send a large flower wreath and a sizable monetary contribution.

The funeral

At the funeral, the family will burn joss paper (or spirit paper) to ensure their loved one has a safe journey to the netherworld. Fake paper money and miniature items like cars, houses, and televisions are burned. These items are sometimes associated with the loved one's interests and are believed to follow them into the afterlife. This way they have everything they need when they enter the spirit world.

A eulogy may be given and, if the person was religious, prayers may also be said.

The family will distribute red envelopes with a coin inside to guests to ensure they return home safely. The family may also give guests a piece of candy that must be consumed that day and before going home. A handkerchief may also be given. The envelope with coin, sweet, and handkerchief should not be taken home.

One final item, a piece of red thread, may be given. The red threads should be taken home and tied to the front doorknobs of the guests' homes to keep evil spirits away.

After the funeral

After the funeral ceremony, a funeral procession to the cemetery or crematorium is held. A hired band resembling a marching band typically leads the procession and plays loud music to frighten spirits and ghosts.

The family wears mourning clothes and walks behind the band. Following the family is the hearse or sedan containing the coffin. It is typically adorned with a large portrait of the deceased hanging on the windshield. Friends and associates complete the procession.

The size of the procession depends on the wealth of the deceased and his or her family. The sons and daughters wear black and white mourning clothes and walk in the front row of the procession. Daughters-in-law come next and also wear black and white clothes. Grandsons and granddaughters wear blue mourning clothes. Professional mourners who are paid to wail and cry are often hired to fill up the procession.

Depending on their personal preference, Chinese were buried or cremated in the past, but now are mainly cremated for environment concern. At a minimum, families make an annual visit to the gravesite on the Qing Ming or Tomb-Sweeping Festival.

Mourners will wear a cloth band on their arms to show that they are in a period of mourning. If the deceased is a man, the band goes on the left sleeve. If the deceased is a woman, the band is pinned to the right sleeve. The mourning band is worn for the duration of the mourning period which can last up to 100 days. Mourners also wear somber clothes. Bright and colorful clothes are avoided during the mourning period.

(Adapted from *thoughtco.com*)

A6. Assignment

Poster Design

Design an English poster on the topic, **my dreaming life course.** The major parts might include:

- A brief introduction of your whole life course.
- Sketch the journey you have completed.
- Design you dreaming life journey left and tell how you will complete it.

Part B Love and Marriage

B1. Introduction

Traditional Chinese Wedding Customs

Traditional Chinese weddings have slowly adopted more contemporary features over the generations. However, certain cherished elements are a fixture in most Chinese weddings which date back centuries. If you're considering becoming engaged or happen to be traveling through China during wedding seasons, you should familiarize yourself with some of these most revered traditions.

Before the wedding

Although Chinese wedding customs varies from area to area, there are essential rituals they have in common. These include proposal making, birthday inquiring, marriage divination, the betrothal gift presentation, wedding date fixing, bridal dowry delivering, and the wedding ceremony itself.

Proposal Making. In ancient times, marriage was completely arranged by the parents of the future bride and groom. When a boy's parents found a prospective bride-to-be, they would send a match-maker to the girl's family to discuss the possibility of the union.

Birthday Inquiring. If the proposal is agreed to by the girl and her family, the boy's parents would send a match-maker to the girl's family to inquire into girl's name and date of birth.

Marriage Divination. The boy's parents would send the name and birth-date of the boy and the girl to a future-teller to see whether their marriage is appropriate.

Betrothal Gift Presenting. Two or three months before the wedding, the bridegroom's family arranges the betrothal gift including betrothal letter, clothes, jewelry, gold, silver and money, and asks the match-maker to present these to the bride's family. This acts as the groom's formal proposal to the bride's family. The bride's family will often agree to entrust their daughter into the groom's care.

During the period between the wedding date settlement and welcoming the bride, the bride's parents will deliver the bride's dowry a few days before the wedding, including pillows, new clothes for the bride in a suitcase, a tea set for the wedding's tea ceremony, two pairs of red wooden clogs, gold jewelry given by bride's parents, etc.

A "return gift" is then given by the bride's family to that of the groom intended to express the wish to uphold positive relations between the in-laws.

Wedding Date Fixing. If the engagement is confirmed, the two families would invite an experienced person to choose a proper wedding date according to tung shing, a Chinese divination guide and almanac. The chosen wedding date is believed to be auspicious, which could bring good luck and happiness to the new couple in the future. Couples typically base their chosen wedding day based on their birthdays and keep away from certain dates and seasons deemed to be unlucky.

A few days before the wedding takes place, the bridal bed will be built and close friends of the bride-to-be will cover it in dried longans, red dates, lotus seeds, persimmon, a sprig of pomegranate leaves, and some money. The bed, once installed, is off-limits to anyone but the married couple.

The night before the big day, both the bride and groom typically undergo a hair-combing ceremony separately in their respective homes. Both bride and groom will first bathe with pomegranate leaves or pomelo to protect them from evil spirits. The two are adorned with new clothing and slippers when they are done. Then a close friend or family member is permitted to comb the hair of the bride and groom.

The hair is combed four times, each time a line of a poem is recited by whomever is doing the combing:

May your marriage last a lifetime,

May you be blessed with a happy and harmonious marriage until old age,

May you be blessed with an abundance of children and grandchildren,

May you be blessed with longevity.

On the wedding day

The wedding ceremony is mainly composed of the following parts:

Welcoming the Bride. On the morning of the wedding day, the groom goes to the bride's home. Younger brides often have a few girlfriends at home who will tease the groom and beg for small gifts or red envelopes stuffed with money before letting him in. Then the groom carries the bride on his back to the sedan chair. Accompanied by boisterous blaring trumpets, the bride is welcomed into the groom's home.

Bowing to Heaven and Earth. Once at the groom's home, the bride and groom bow to heaven and earth in front of the groom's family altar first, the groom's parents second, and to each other last.

Traditional Tea Ceremony. At the groom's home, the couple offers tea to their elders including the groom's parents. The elder's acceptance of the tea indicates that the family has welcomed the bride into the groom's family.

After the wedding

On the day after the wedding, the bride wakes up early and pays a visit to the groom's relatives. It is only then that she is formally introduced to the groom's relatives, while the bride would receive small gifts from the groom's relatives.

Three days after the wedding, the bride and bridegroom will pay a visit to the bride's family, at which point the bride would be received as a guest as opposed to a member of her former family.

In some areas of China, these traditional Chinese wedding customs still exist. If you are lucky enough, you may see a traditional Chinese wedding ceremony during your China tours, which would be an extremely interesting experience on your trip.

(Adapted from *Chinatour.com*)

B2. Words and Expressions

Vocabulary

1. sedan /sɪˈdæn/ *n*. (可以搭载四五个人,有两个或四个门,后部有专门放置行李空间的)轿车
2. couplet /ˈkʌplət/ *n*. (尤指长度、韵脚相同的)对句
3. embroidered /ɪmˈbrɔɪdəd/ *adj*. 绣花的;刺绣的
4. chaplet /ˈtʃæplət/ *n*. (用叶、花或珠宝做成的)花冠
5. robe /rəʊb/ *n*. 长袍,罩袍;(尤指特别正式场合穿的)袍服,礼袍
6. conjugal /ˈkaːndʒəgəl/ *adj*. 婚姻的
7. felicity /fəˈlɪsəti/ *n*. 幸福;幸运
8. divine /dɪˈvaɪn/ *adj*. 神的;像神一样的; 极好的
9. eternal /ɪˈtɜːnəl/ *adj*. 永远的,永恒的;长期的

婚礼用品与象征寓意	Wedding Items and Symbolic Meanings
花轿	a bridal sedan chair
“囍”字	Hanzi “Xi” / double happiness
龙凤联	dragon and phoenix couplet
龙凤烛	dragon and phoenix candles
崭新的红色床上用品	brand new red bedclothes
刺绣棉被	embroidered quilt
红盖头	red head cover
头饰	headdress / headwear
凤冠霞帔	a chaplet and official robes
头纱	veil
胸花	brooch
旗袍	cheongsam
婚纱,嫁衣	bridal gowns
百年好合	lifetime of conjugal felicity
早生贵子	early birth
佳偶天成	perfect match like is arranged by divines
天作之合	perfect couple arranged by heaven
举案齐眉	mutual respect in a marriage
同心同德	alike heart, faith, and goal
天长地久	eternal as heaven and earth
喜结连理	tie the knot
梳发礼寓意长寿、忠诚、多子女和好运	combing hair rites symbolizes longevity, loyalty, many children, and good luck
红烛同时熄灭象征白头偕老	the candles burning off at the same time symbolizes living happily together until hair turned grey
红色象征幸运和财富	red symbolizes luck and good fortune
莲子象征多子多福	lotus seed symbolizes many children and many blessings

Vocabulary

1. broker /ˈbrəʊkə/ *n.* 经纪人;(尤指政府的)中间人
2. horoscope /ˈhɔːrəskəʊp/ *n.* 星相;占星预测
3. divination /dɪvəˈneɪʃən/ *n.* 占卜,算命
4. lament /ləˈment/ *v.* 对……感到悲痛,对……表示失望,痛惜

传统婚嫁	**Traditional Marriage**
父母之命,媒妁之言	listen to the marriage broker and obey the command of the parents
先成家后立业	get married before starting one's career
头等大事	the biggest event
生辰八字	birth horoscope
三书六礼	the Three Letters and Six Etiquettes
婚书,婚约	a marriage contract
纳彩	the proposal
问名	ask for information
纳吉	divination
纳征	send betrothal gifts
请期	decide wedding date
亲迎	the wedding ceremony
月老	Yue Lao
媒人,媒婆	match-maker / marriage broker
安床	arrange the new couple's bed

Vocabulary

1. click /klɪk/ *v*. 点击;(使)发出咔嗒声 *n*. 短而尖的声音
2. destined /ˈdestɪnd/ *adj*. 命中注定的,命运决定的
3. unrequited /ˌʌnrɪˈkwaɪtɪd/ *adj*. (爱情)单方面的,得不到回报的,单相思的
4. cyber /saɪbə/ *adj*. 计算机的;与电脑有关的;网络的(尤指因特网)
5. gathering /ˈɡæðəɪŋ/ *n*. 聚会;集会

现代爱情	**Modern Love**
男女平等	gender equality
单身人士	singles / singletons
一见钟情	click together
日久生情	a growing love
天赐良缘	destined to be a happy match
自由恋爱	free love
暗恋	unrequited love

谈恋爱,有浪漫关系	be in a relationship
与某人约会	go out with someone
异地恋	long distance relationship
分手	break up
失恋	be crossed in love
相亲	blind date
相亲市场	dating market / marriage market
联谊会	social gatherings
扩大交友圈	expand one's social circles
交友软件	dating apps
交友网站	dating websites
情人节	Valentine's Day
七夕节	Chinese Valentine's Day
情侣装	his-and-hers clothes

Vocabulary

1. prenuptial /ˌpriːˈnʌpʃəl/ *adj*. 结婚前的
2. bureau /ˈbjʊrəʊ/ *n*. (政府部门的)局,处,科
3. monogamy /məˈnɑːgəmi/ *n*. 一夫一妻制
4. marital /ˈmerɪtəl/ *adj*. 婚姻的

现代婚嫁	**Modern Marriage**
法定结婚年龄	marriageable age
婚介服务	matchmaking service
婚前协议	prenuptial agreement
男子婚前单身派对(仅男性参与)	stag nights
民政局	civil affairs bureau
婚姻登记处	marriage registration office
拍结婚照	take wedding photos
登记成配偶	signing the register
结婚证	marriage certificate
一夫一妻制	monogamy
晚婚	marry late

裸婚	naked marriage
婚姻状况	marital status
计划生育	family planning
二孩政策	two-child policy
三孩政策	three-child policy
结婚周年纪念日	wedding anniversary

Vocabulary

1. reciprocate /rɪˈsɪprəkeɪt/ *v*. 回报,报答,酬答
2. proposal /prəˈpəʊzəl/ *n*. 建议;计划;提案;求婚
3. betrothal /bɪˈtrəʊðəl/ *n*. 婚约;订婚
4. engaged /ɪnˈgeɪdʒd/ *adj*. 已订婚的;卷入……的;从事……的;忙于某事的
5. auspicious /ɑːˈspɪʃəs/ *adj*. 吉利的;吉祥的

订婚事项	**Engagement Matters**
彩礼	bride price
嫁妆	dowry
回礼	reciprocate with gifts
配偶	spouse
准新娘	would-be bride
准新郎	would-be groom
未婚妻	fiancee
未婚夫	fiance
求婚	proposal making
提亲	propose marriage
聘书	betrothal letter
礼书	gift letter
迎书	wedding letter
订婚	get engaged to
订婚戒指	engagement ring
婚纱照	wedding photo
挑选良辰吉日	choose an auspicious date
婚期	wedding day

Vocabulary

1. march /maːrtʃ/ *n.* 示威游行；进行曲；(尤指)行军
2. newlywed /ˈnuːliwed/ *n.* 新婚者
3. matrimonial /ˌmætrəˈməʊnɪəl/ *adj.* 婚姻的
4. chamber /ˈtʃeɪmbə/ *n.* 会议厅；房间，室
5. banter /ˈbæntə/ *v.* (善意地)取笑，逗弄

婚礼流程	**Wedding Celebrations / Festivities**
司仪	wedding master of ceremony
合法夫妻	legally wedded couple
新郎	groom
新娘	bride
伴郎	best men
伴娘	bridesmaid
婆婆 / 岳母	mother-in-law
公公 / 岳父	father-in-law
亲朋好友	near and dear ones
邀请函	the invitation
婚礼进行曲	the wedding march
喜糖	wedding candies
为新人铺床	arrange the newlyweds' bed
婚床	matrimonial bed
梳头礼	comb hair rites
红包	red packet
礼单簿	register
敲锣打鼓	play the gong and the drum
向新娘的父母告别	bid farewell to the bride's parents
敬茶礼	wedding's tea ceremony
奉茶	to present tea to their parents
喝喜酒	attend a wedding banquet
主桌	top table
敬酒	toast to friends and relatives
拜堂；三拜礼	Three Bow Ceremony

拜天地,拜高堂,夫妻对拜	bow to heaven and earth / parents / each other
喝交杯酒	drink cross-cupped wine
回门	go back to the bride's parents' place / Hui Men
度蜜月	go for a honeymoon holiday

B3. Speaking Activities

Situational Speech

Imagine that you are an international student, and your teacher Miss Gale is about to hold a wedding ceremony. Interested in wedding culture, she asks each student to deliver a speech toward **wedding tradition in my hometown.** Prepare a 5-minute speech. Your speech might cover:

- Traditional wedding customs in your hometown, like marriage price, dowry, and wedding clothes.
- What impressed you most in your personal experiences of attending a wedding?
- What kind of wedding ceremony do you dream to have, why?

You may refer to the words and expressions in Part B, but don't confine yourself to them.

Role Play

Imagine that you work as a professional wedding planner. One day, a new couple comes to your studio and asks you to **design a wedding with traditional Chinese characteristics.** You need to tell the details of the plan. Your introduction might include:

- How will you decorate the wedding setting?
- The food and drink that will be served at the wedding.
- Major activities along the wedding.
- The things that will be used at the wedding.
- Whether to add western elements to the wedding.

Brainstorming

Traditionally, Chinese people hold a marvelous wedding ceremony to share their happiness. But with the development of society, some people choose to simplify their wedding, which means newlyweds only invite the nearest and dearest to their wedding and the wedding process is less complicated. Some people even skip the wedding and select to spend their money on honeymoon. So how do you view simplified weddings and no wedding, and how will you celebrate your own wedding in the future? Brainstorm and share your opinions with your class.

Read and Share

Read the following paragraphs about the **blind date, which is considered as** one way to find true love, and share your views.

Paragraph 1

Parents find their children blind dates in parks. "Spouse-hunting fairs held by parents who are eager to see their children tie the knot have made parks in China a heaven for relationship hunters and their parents". Zhongshan Park has been the location for six years where parents go to seek partners for their children. This process begins with the parents sitting on a bench with their child's credentials, such as photos and academic or career information. After the information has been exchanged and the parents like what they see, questions are asked about anything ranging from their child's zodiac sign to their place of residence. If everything runs smoothly during the second step, contact information is exchanged.

(Adapted from *altwiki.org*)

Paragraph 2

Today, most blind dates aren't totally blind per se, as thanks to online social sites, many people have photographs of themselves online that are easily accessible by others. Dates arranged through personal ads may still be blind if no photos or last names are exchanged. In this type of blind date, a phone call or two as well as first names are often exchanged before a meeting is arranged in a public place such as a cafe.

(Adapted from *wise-geek.com*)

Please conduct a team discussion, and share ideas upon the topics:

- Will you accept a blind date arranged by your parents? Why?
- Do you believe cyber love is a good way to find true love?
- Is it necessary to have an online chat before a blind date?

Debate

To go Dutch, also known as a Dutch treat or a Dutch date, implies an informal agreement for each person to pay for his or her own expenses during a planned date or outing. The decision to do this is usually made in advance in order to avoid any confusion when the bill arrives or the tickets are purchased. Under certain social and financial circumstances, the idea allows larger groups of friends or co-workers to enjoy a night without the worry of one host footing the entire bill. During a romantic dating situation, however, the suggestion to go Dutch may not be as well received.

(Adapted from *infobloom.com*)

Topic for Debate:

As we all know, women are becoming more and more independent with the change of the times. At the same time, blind date becomes quite common, and usually the expense of a blind date can be costly. So do you approve of **going Dutch on a blind date**?

Interpretation

Use the words and expressions you learned from Part B of this unit to interpret the paragraphs below into English.

Paragraph 1

近年来,传统中式婚礼在国内越来越受年轻人的欢迎。中式婚礼有许多繁琐的程序,每个环节都蕴含着美好的寓意。婚礼现场张灯结彩,洋溢着喜庆的氛围。舞台上,新人会进行三拜礼:拜天地、拜高堂、对拜。接着便是敬茶礼,通常在敬茶礼之后新人会从双方父母那收到一个红包。典型的中式婚礼流程一般还包括喝交杯酒,表示从此合为一体,彼此恩爱,同甘共苦。

Paragraph 2

订婚是在结婚前举行的一场仪式,用来证明双方的恋爱关系,表明双方的关系向婚礼迈进了。虽然现在是自由恋爱的时代,但对于结婚这样的终身大事,一般还需征求父母长辈的建议。订婚仪式前,男方会将聘礼送到女方家里,聘礼的数量不论多少,但必须是吉利的数字,而女方也会回礼。另外,双方家长还需要挑选出良辰吉日来举办仪式,确定宾客名单。在订婚宴上,准新郎和准新娘一般会交换订婚戒指、致辞并向宾客敬酒。在某些情况下,准新郎和准新娘还会签订婚书留作纪念。

Paragraph 3

随着时代的发展,许多历史糟粕已被摒弃,一夫多妻制被一夫一妻制取代,包办婚姻被自由恋爱取代。在自由恋爱中,有些人是一见钟情,有些人则是日久生情,但只要两情相悦,便是最好的感情。对于单身人士来说,相较于虚拟的交友软件,相亲是一个更加高效且稳妥的寻找伴侣的方式,因为中间人会提前告知双方相亲对象的基本信息。如果相亲双方对彼此都满意的话,他们就可以开始约会了。

B4. Culture Highlights

> **Q:** *Betrothal gift is one of the marriage customs in China, which is used to express the groom's gratitude toward the parents of the bride. However, expensive gifts can be economic and mental burdens for parents, so what measures have been taken to get rid of bad customs?*
>
> **A:** North China's Hebei province has chosen five areas as experimental zones for reforming wedding customs, aiming to curb extravagance and waste in marriage

practices and encouraging simple and civilized wedding conventions.

The areas include Xiong'an New Area, a new economic zone to receive Beijing's non-capital functions, Xinji city and some districts in different cities of the province.

The list was approved by the province's Department of Civil Affairs on Monday and the experimental period for the pilot areas will be three years.

During this time, some former practices adopted by Chinese in weddings will be reduced, such as high-price betrothal gifts from the bridegroom to the bride's family, extravagance and waste in wedding receptions, and vulgar behavior that targets making fun of newlyweds, the department said.

It added that the pilot areas' mission is to establish a new wedding custom which is healthy, civilized, simple, and appropriate while keeping some good traditions.

(Adapted from *chinadaily.com*)

Q: *In traditional Chinese wedding, people prefer red rather than white, why?*

A: Red, the color of love, symbolizes romance, and enthusiasm in Western culture. Wearing a red wedding dress is going to show the world your passionate and brave personality on your big day.

Moreover, in Chinesc culture, red is a traditionally auspicious color that represents joy and celebration. It is widely used in festivals and special events such as weddings. Wearing red wedding dresses has been a Chinese wedding tradition since the Ming Dynasty over 650 years ago. In Chinese culture, the bride wears a red wedding dress such as a Qun Kwa or a cheongsam on her wedding day to celebrate the joy and happiness of the marriage.

However, in Chinese culture, white is not as desirable of a color for a wedding dress because it represents death and sadness. Traditionally, people believe that wearing white to a wedding brings bad luck. In spite of its traditional meaning, due to the influence of Western culture, more and more modern brides have embraced the simplicity and purity of white wedding dresses and have chosen to wear them on their wedding day. Today, many brides even consider wearing a white modern Chinese cheongsam to combine their two cultures.

(Adapted from *eastmeetsdress.com*)

Q: *People say Yue Lao is equivalent to the god of love, why?*

A: To the ancient Chinese, love was not defined by a goddess, but destined by Yue Lao's red silken threads. Known best from the tale, the Old Man Under the Moon, Yue Lao's story has endured for almost a thousand years, and star struck lovers still seek his blessing today.

The ancient Chinese were firm believers in fate, certain that their days were recorded and foretold before they were born. This included the belief that couples were destined to be together. It is in Yue Lao's *Book of Marriages* that the names of future couples were recorded, and it is Yue Lao that bound potential couples together with his red silken string.

In Chinese mythology, Yue Lao is known as the god of love and marriage. Yue Lao is an immortal and is believed to live on the moon, while other legends claim he lives in the "obscure regions" near the underworld. And while his story has persisted for over one thousand years, he is still actively prayed to today.

Unlike other cultures that feature women as goddesses of love, in Chinese mythology it is an old man, Yue Lao, that is the god of love and marriage.

In legends, Yue Lao appears at night and carries a mysterious *Book of Marriages* Yue Xia Lao Ren carries a pack of red string which he often holds in hands and rubs between his fingers, which he uses to tie the feet of couples destined to be together Once names are found in the *Book of Marriages* and connected, what is written will come to pass.

Belief in Yue Lao still exists, and it is customary for couples to wear red bracelets to signify their commitment.

More than just a Chinese version of Cupid, Yue Lao's power is still sought after today. What fate puts together none can tear asunder. To have Yue Lao's blessing, is powerful indeed.

(Adapted from *timelessmyths.com*)

B5. Extension

Synonym Discrimination

Can you figure out the differences among the words and phrases below?

Group 1: bridal / nuptial / conjugal / married / marital / matrimonial / marriageable
Group 2: date / appointment / engagement
Group 3: ceremony / celebration / ritual / rite / party

Extensive Reading

Passage One

Bride's Home Visit

Traditionally the bride's home visit is three days after the Chinese wedding ceremony. For efficiency, modern Chinese wedding usually compressed all the necessary events into a single day.

One costume change equals three days!

After the tea ceremony at the groom's family home, the bride will change out of her western style wedding gown. This change of clothes symbolizes the passing of three days!

The bride may choose to change into another western dress, a cheongsam or a traditional red Chinese wedding gown called kwa.

The kwa is made of silk, heavily embroidered with motifs of dragon, phoenix and flowers in gold and silver threads. Although heavy due to the embroidery, it is cool and comfortable to wear. The jacket is straight cut and the straight skirt is usually elasticized at the waist.

What a joy to relax in the loose cut of the kwa for a few hours before getting back into that body hugging western style wedding gown for the wedding banquet!

Bride's younger brother to escort the bride home

The bride's younger brother (or whoever is playing the role) will arrive at the groom's home with a wedding basket filled with toiletries, perfumed oils, make-up, etc for his sister. He misses his sister and wants her to go back with him for a visit.

The bridal car will fetch the bride's younger brother to the groom's home. The groom will welcome the younger brother by opening the car door for him.

She is definitely not going home empty handed!

The bride's home visit is the couple's first visit to her parent's home as a married couple. The bride cannot go back empty handed.

Other than the gifts for her parents, the couple was supposed to prepare gifts for all the elder members of the family. Nowadays, red packets are used instead.

Chickens to lead the way!

In the past, many dialect groups required the bride to return home with gifts of a pair of sugar cane, a pair of live rooster and hen for her parents. These "dai lu ji" were supposed to lead the way back.

In return, the bride's parents will also provide gifts of a rooster and hen. These will be put under the bridal bed back at the groom's home. It was believed that the firstborn will be male if the rooster came out first.

Over the years as the standard of living improved the live chickens were replaced by other types of meat, poultry, fish and expensive dried or gourmet food items such as abalone, birdnest, or shark fin.

To simplify matters most of these gifts are no longer required for modern Chinese weddings or are simply replaced by red packets.

Roast pig and peanut candies

Nowadays, only symbolic items such as the roast pig or candies are requested by brides' parents.

If one of the bride's parents is Cantonese, the roast pig is definitely required as part of the gifts for the bride's home visit. For non-Cantonese, sometimes roast pork instead of a whole roast pig is requested.

For teochew, two big red packets of their favorite traditional peanut and sesame candies "dou tiao, zi ma tiao" are usually requested.

For hokkiens, combinations of popped rice blocks, or popped rice and sesame rolls, peanut chewy candies, bean paste cookies "mi fang, ma lao, gong tang, dou sa bing" are usually requested.

Tangerines and oranges too!

Tangerines or mandarin oranges "Juzi" sounds like good fortune "Ji" in Chinese and must be included as part of the gifts. If tangerines are out of season, oranges can be used instead.

More is better!

Ensure that the quantity of the items is sufficient for a portion to be returned to signify sharing of fortune between the two families. Tangerines or oranges will have to be replaced in the returned gifts.

Tea ceremony during the bride's home visit

The groom is introduced to the bride's family at the tea ceremony during the bride's home visit.

The bride's mother's wedding tea set, if available, is used for this ceremony.

Otherwise, any nice tea set can be used.

The order of service is the same as the tea ceremony at the groom's home.

Usually the relatives of the bride will present her with jewellery rather than red packets. This is referred to as adding to her dowry "tien jia zhuang".

Sweet soup for a sweet union

During the bride's home visit, a sweet soup with lotus seeds, dried longan, red dates and rice balls will be served to wish the couple a sweet harmonious marriage.

The modern Chinese wedding ceremony is completed after the bride's home visit. The wedding banquet may be on the same day or another day as it is just an announcement and celebration of the marriage.

(Adapted from *chinese-wedding-guide.com*)

Passage Two

Confinement after Childbirth

Confinement after childbirth is a traditional practice in Asian countries where Chinese mothers would stay indoors at home for a full month after giving birth. Mums going for caesarean section require longer confinement period for recovery than natural birth. As an overview, confinement preparation is usually arranged 3 to 6 months before pregnant woman goes into labour. While western confinement is more of taking care of baby angels, there is a set of do's and don'ts rules for Asian new mothers to follow.

Confinement food delivery to home, hiring day time confinement lady or 24 hour stay in nanny are much sought after for mum's confinement in Singapore. Unless you have experience and know what to do during confinement period, getting a confinement nanny or pui yuet is recommended. Other "quarantined" options can be hospitals, confinement centres and luxury confinement hotels if you are staying in Malaysia. It is a choice preference of your privacy whether you are comfortable with stranger to your home, 1 to 1 private care and availability of extra rooms.

Chinese confinement myths

According to Chinese beliefs, confinement rules and practices are meant for the benefit of mother and prevent bad things from happening. Chinese postpartum traditions include preparing nutritious confinement meals with herbs, no bathing, no washing of hair, no drinking of water and no outdoors. Most traditional confinement nannies would advise on following the Chinese custom. However, with today's medical advancement, some confinement taboos and restrictions are considered confinement myths which are not necessary to follow strictly.

Confinement nanny

New parents will not know what to do after giving birth especially with twins. Non-stop baby crying can be a daunting experience. Someone with real life practical experience of post natal care is essential. Many families in Singapore still prefer to engage confinement nannies even for their second birth in order to be well rested with good health recovery. Experienced confinement nanny provides first time parents a better peace of mind and security. She will take care of the meals, washing clothes and most importantly, waking up to baby at night for breastfeeding or diaper changing. Highly recommended if it is your first time parenthood for a happy and smooth transition. Confinement period can be extended if help and care is required after 28 days, up to a maximum of 16 weeks calculated from the child's date of birth. However, the extension will depend on the availability of nanny as usually their appointments are pre-booked. To avoid disappointment in not able to continue with the same nanny, parents are advised to pre-arrange with confinement agency if help for more than 28 days is foreseen.

Confinement food

What to eat after giving birth is important for new mums to boost milk supply, recover their health and reset their body condition. Extra precaution with cold water, cooling food, cold air or windy environment must be taken to prevent mum from catching chill or cold. That is why ingredients such as Chinese herbs, gingers are used during cooking to warm mum's body, recover her Qi and balance her energy. Mums are advised to avoid food that is chili spicy, oily, salty, and MSG as well. For more convenience, mums can buy pre packed confinement herbs for soup or confinement food catering services to take care of the daily meals.

Confinement herbal package

Getting a confinement herbal package is more economical and convenient compared to buying herbs individually. It is ideal and essential during postpartum period with or without a confinement nanny. The 28 days confinement package would include confinement herbal bath, red dates for making tea and pre packed confinement herbs for soup. You can buy confinement herbs packages from HockHua, Eu Yan Sang, Bugis or confinement nanny agency of your confinement lady.

Post Natal Massage

During postpartum confinement, mums should consider post natal home massage for mind, body relaxation after the physical, emotional tolls of pregnancy and labour. Post natal massage is suitable for premature delivery, normal delivery or C-section delivery. The home massage therapy ses sions include massage of the breasts, unclogging blocked milk ducts and engorgement. A minimum of 5 to 10 consecutive days of Jamu massage with binding are required in order to see the effectiveness. Start date for normal delivery is 5 days after childbirth. However, start date for caesarean section needs to depend on the recovery stage of mummy's wound as every woman is different and has a different recovery rate. It is usually 3 weeks to 4 weeks and a clearance from Gynae is required in order to proceed with the massage for caesarean section.

(Adapted from *nannysos.com.sg*)

B6. Assignment

Invitation Design

Design an English wedding invitation. All wedding invitations should include the following elements:

- Who's hosting?
- The request to come to the wedding.
- The names of the couple.
- The date and time.
- The location.

References

DR. Armstrong. (2019). The Twelve Stages of the Human Life Cycle. *American Institute for Learning and Human Development*. Retrieved from https://www.institute4learning.com/resources/articles/the-12-stages-of-life/ on January 29th, 2022.

The Coming of Age Ceremony in Ancient China. *VisitBeijing.com.cn*. Retrieved from http://english.visitbeijing.com.cn/a1/a-XB3V7K0E6C7DCDD78CD1B7 on January 29th, 2022.

Coming of Age Ceremony in Chinese Culture. *China Fetching*. Retrieved from https://www.chinafetching.com/coming-of-age on January 29th, 2022.

Joe Oliveto. (2020). Chinese Ancestor Worship Explained: History, Traditions & More. *Joincake*. Retrieved from https://www.joincake.com/blog/chinese-ancestor-worship/#:~:text=%20Chinese%20Ancestor%20Worship%20Traditions%20%26%20Rituals%20,another%20example%20of%20a%20way%20many...%20More%20 on January 29th, 2022.

Cathy Wu. (2021). Explainer: Everything You Need to Know About the Gaokao.

Thatsmags. Retrieved from https://www.thatsmags.com/china/post/13965/explainer-gaokao on January 29th, 2022.

Death Around the World: Chinese Funeral Customs and Traditions. *FuneralGuide*. Retrieved from https://www.funeralguide.co.uk/blog/death-around-world-chinese-funeral-customs-and-traditions on January 29th, 2022.

Charles Custer. (2019). Chinese Birthday Customs for the Elderly. *ThoughtCo*. Retrieved from https://www.thoughtco.com/chinese-birthday-customs-for-the-elderly-4082746 on January 29th, 2022.

Gavin. (2022). Fortune Telling in China. *Chinahighlights*. Retrieved from https://www.chinahighlights.com/travelguide/article-fortune-telling.htm on February 12th, 2022.

Yeo, Teresa Rebecca. (2013). Chinese Birth Rituals. *Infopedia*. Retrieved from https://eresources.nlb.gov.sg/infopedia/articles/SIP_2013-05-14_113920.html on January 29th, 2022.

Lauren Mack. (2020). Chinese Funeral Traditions. *ThoughtCo*. Retrieved from https://www.thoughtco.com/chinese-funeral-traditions-687456 on January 29th, 2022.

Meila Mertz. (2013). Traditional Chinese Wedding Customs. *Chinatour*. Retrieved from https://www.chinatour.com/discover-traditional-chinese-wedding-customs/ on January 29th, 2022.

Sheri Cyprus. (2022). What Is a Blind Date? *Wise-geek*. Retrieved from https://www.wise-geek.com/what-is-a-blind-date.htm on January 29th, 2022.

Michael Pollick. (2022). What does It Mean When You "Go Dutch"? *Infobloom*. Retrieved from https://www.infobloom.com/what-does-it-mean-when-you-go-dutch.htm#:~:text=To%20go%20Dutch%2C%20also%20known%20as%20a%20Dutch, the%20bill%20arrives%20or%20the%20tickets%20are%20purchased on January 29th, 2022.

Zhang Yu. (2021). China's Hebei to Pilot Reformed Wedding Customs. *China Daily*. Retrieved from http://www.chinadaily.com.cn/a/202105/26/WS60ae3450a31024ad0bac1a1f.html on January 29th, 2022.

Wedding Dress Color Meanings for Modern Chinese Weddings. *Eastmeetsdress*. Retrieved from https://eastmeetsdress.com/blogs/blog/wedding-dress-color-meanings-for-modern-chinese-weddings on January 29th, 2022.

Yue Lao: The Ancient Chinese God of Love and Marriage. *Timelessmyths*. Retrieved from https://www.timelessmyths.com/gods/chinese/yue-lao/ on January 29th, 2022.

Bride's home visit. *chinese-wedding-guide*. Retrieved from http://www.chinese-wedding-guide.com/brides-home-visit.html on January 29th, 2022.

Confinement After Childbirth. *nannysos*. Retrieved from https://www.nannysos.com.sg/confinement-after-childbirth/ on January 29th, 2022.

Unit 3 Creativity and Communication

Part A Creativity

A1. Introduction

Top 20 Ancient Chinese Inventions

Ancient China held leading positions in many fields in studying nature in the world. Besides the four great inventions — papermaking, printing, gunpowder and the compass, ancient China contributed countless other inventions to the world. How many other creations do you know? Below is a list of the 20 inventions created by ancient Chinese and some may surprise you.

Papermaking

The invention of paper greatly affects human history. Paper already existed in China since 105 BC, however, a eunuch named Cai Lun made significant innovation and helped drive its widespread adoption. His advanced paper-making technology then spread to central Asia and the world through the Silk Road.

Movable type printing

Woodblock printing was already a widely used technique in the Tang Dynasty. However, this kind of printing tech was expensive and time-consuming. In the Song Dynasty (960-1279), a man named Bi Sheng invented movable type printing, making it quicker and easier. He first carved individual characters on pieces of clay and then hardened them with fire. These movable type pieces were later glued to an iron plate to print a page and then broken up and redistributed for another page. This kind of printing tech rapidly spread across Europe, leading up to the Renaissance, and later all around the world.

Gunpowder

Gunpowder was invented by Chinese Taoist alchemists when they tried to find a potion to gain human immortality by mixing elemental sulfur, charcoal and saltpeter. By 1044 there were several formulas for creating gunpowder in China. It was quickly worked out that it could be used as a weapon. Gunpowder did not start to appear in Europe for almost another two hundred years.

Compass

A compass is a navigational instrument that shows directions. The compass was invented by Chinese between the 2nd century BC and 1st century AD. It was first used in *fengshui*, the layout of buildings. By 1000 AD, navigational compasses were commonly used on Chinese ships, enabling them to navigate. Arab traders sailing to China learned of the tech and brought it to the West.

Alcohol

The inhabitants of the Arabian Peninsula were widely believed to be the first brewers. However, in 2013, a 9000-year-old pottery found in Henan province revealed the presence of alcohol, 1000 years before Arabian. Alcohol is known as *jiu* in Chinese and is often used as offerings to Heaven and the Earth or ancestors in ancient China. Study shows that beer with an alcoholic content of 4% to 5% was widely consumed in ancient China and was even mentioned on oracle bone inscriptions of the Shang Dynasty (1600 BC-1046 BC).

Mechanical clock

The world's first mechanical clock — Water-driven Spherical Birds — was invented by Yi Xing, a Buddhist monk in 725 AD. It was operated by dripping water which powered a wheel that made one revolution in 24 hours. Hundreds of years later, the inventor Su Song developed a more sophisticated clock called the Cosmic Empire in 1092, 200 years earlier before the mechanical clock was created in Europe.

Tea production

According to old Chinese legend, tea was first discovered by Shennong, Chinese Father of Agriculture. In the Tang Dynasty (618-907), tea became a popular drink enjoyed by all social classes. *Cha Jing* (or *The Book of Tea*), written by Lu Yu in the Tang Dynasty, explicated ways to cultivate tea, tea drinking and different classifications of tea in details. The book is considered as the world's first monograph about tea. And the world's oldest and largest living tea tree can be found in Lin Cang, China, about 3,200 years old.

Silk

Silk, one of the oldest fibers, originated in China as early as 6,000 years ago. The earliest evidence of silk was discovered at Yangshao culture site in Xiaxian County, Shanxi Province, where a silk cocoon was found cut in half, dating back to between 4000 and 3000 BC. Chinese people mastered sophisticated silk weaving technique, and the West had to pay gold of the same weight for the silk. For many centuries businessmen transported this precious item from China to the West, forming the famous Silk Road.

Umbrella

The invention of umbrella can be traced back as early as 3500 years ago in China. Legend has it that Lu Ban, a Chinese carpenter and inventor, created the first umbrella. Inspired by children using lotus leaves as rain shelter, he created umbrella by making a flexible framework covered by a cloth.

Acupuncture

The oldest Chinese medicine book *Neijing*, also known as *The Classic of Internal Medicine of the Yellow Emperor*, shows that acupuncture was widely used as a therapy in China much before the time it was written. Besides, various kinds of acupuncture needles were discovered in the tomb of Prince Liu Sheng who died around 200 BC. This is a further proof that acupuncture was already in use in China more than two thousand years ago.

Iron smelting

Archaeological evidence revealed that iron smelting technology was developed in China as early as 5th century BC in the Zhou Dynasty (1050 BC-256 BC). During the Spring & Autumn and Warring States periods (776 BC-221 BC), China went into a flourishing period for iron smelting.

Porcelain

Porcelain is a great invention of ancient China. The earliest porcelain emerged in the Shang Dynasty (1600-1046 BC) and matured during the Tang Dynasty (618-906). During the Song Dynasty (960-1279), porcelain production technology reached an unprecedented height due to its focus on shape and the tactile experiences of the glaze. Chinese porcelain was highly prized in the world and many artworks had been introduced to the West through the Silk Road.

Earthquake detector

According to court records of the later Han Dynasty, a seismograph was created by the brilliant inventor Zhang Heng in 132. Its function is to determine the direction of an earthquake. In 138, this instrument indicated an earthquake occurring in Longxi a thousand kilometers away. It was the first time for mankind to detect an earthquake.

Rocket

China is hometown of rockets. Ancient Chinese inventors created rockets by applying counter-force produced by ignited gunpowder. According to history, in 228 the Wei State already used torches attached to arrows to guard Chencang against the invading troops of the Shu State. Later the Song Dynasty (960-1279) adapted gunpowder to make rockets. A paper tube stuffed with gunpowder was attached to an arrow which can be launched by a bow. This kind of ancient rockets and improved ones were widely used in military and entertainment activities in China.

Bronze

The skill of bronze production was mastered by ancient Chinese by 1700 BC. The Shang Dynasty (1600-1046 BC) and the Zhou dynasties (1046-256 BC) brought China into the Bronze Age and the making of bronze wares reached its peak in this period. Bronze was mainly used to make weapons, bronze tools and ritual vessels at that time. Compared to their counterparts in other regions of the world, the Chinese bronze wares stand out for their inscriptions and delicate decorative patterns.

The kite

The kite was developed around 3,000 years ago by ancient Chinese. The earliest kites were made of wood, called *Mu yuan* (wooden kite). In early times kites were mainly used for military purposes such as sending a message, measuring distances, testing the wind and signaling. Over time kite flying developed into playthings and kite flying is now enjoyed worldwide.

The seed drill

The seed drill is a device that plants the seed into soil at a uniform depth and covers it. According to records, the invention of seed drills can be dated back to the 2nd century BC. The device made farmers' job easier and highly improved the agricultural output in China.

Row crop farming

While farmers still scattered seed onto the fields randomly in other parts of the world, ancient Chinese started planting crops in rows from the 6th century BC. They planted individual seeds in rows, thus reducing seed loss and making crops grow faster and stronger. This technology was not used in the western world until 2200 years later.

Toothbrush

The bristle toothbrush was invented in 1498 by the ancient Chinese who made toothbrushes with coarse horse hairs attached to bone or bamboo handles. It was later brought to the new world by the Europeans.

Paper money

Paper money were first developed by the ancient Chinese, who started using folding money at the end of the 8th or beginning of the 9th century. Paper bills were originally used as privately issued bills of credit or exchange notes. A merchant could deposit his cash in the capital, receiving a paper "exchange certificate" which he could exchange for metal coins in other cities.

(Adapted from *Chinawhisper.com*)

A2. Words and Expressions

Vocabulary

1. stalk /stɔːk/ *n*. (植物的)茎,秆
2. blade /bleɪd/ *n*. 肩胛骨,肩胛
3. reeling /riːlɪŋ/ *n*. 摇纱;缫丝
4. bark /bɑːk/ *n*. 树皮
5. hemp /hemp/ *n*. 麻类植物
6. mulberry /ˈmʌlberi/ *n*. 桑树,桑葚
7. bast /bæst/ *n*. 树的内皮
8. durable /ˈdʊrəb(ə)l / *adj*. 持久的,耐用的

造纸术	**Papermaking**
各种天然材料	various natural materials
稻草秆	grass stalk
树叶	tree leaf
兽皮	animal skin
羊皮	sheep skin
岩石	rocks
瓦板	earthen plate
竹条或木条	bamboo or wooden strips
龟壳	tortoise shells

牛肩胛骨	shoulder blades of an ox
记录重要事件	record important events
竹简书	books written on bamboo strips
占据很大空间	take up lots of space
缫丝	silk reeling
帛	*Bo*, a kind of paper made of silk
朝廷	imperial court
因材料稀缺而昂贵	expensive due to the scarcity of materials
纸浆;浆状物	pulp
树皮	tree bark
旧破布	old rags
渔网	fishing nets
麦秆	wheat stalks
桑皮纤维	mulberry fibers
韧皮纤维	bast fibers
平面编织布	flat woven cloth
排干(水)	drain out (water)
干透	dry out
轻质的,轻量的	lightweight
便宜、轻、薄、耐用	cheap, light, thin, durable
适合毛笔书写	suitable for brush writing

Vocabulary

1. manuscript /ˈmænjuskrɪpt/ *n*. 手稿;手抄本
2. sutra /ˈsuːtrə/ *n*. 佛经(等于 sutta);箴言
3. time-consuming /ˈtaɪm kənsuːmɪŋ/ *adj*. 耗时的;旷日持久的
4. engrave /ɪnˈgreɪv/ *v*. 雕刻(文字,图案)
5. ceramic /səˈræmɪk/ *adj*. 陶瓷的
6. moistened /ˈmɔɪsnd/ *adj*. 弄湿的;潮湿的
7. dissemination /dɪˌsemɪˈneɪʃn/ *n*. 宣传;散播

印刷术	**Printing Techniques**
活字印刷术	movable type printing
可重复使用的	reusable
泥活字印刷	clay-type printing
口口相传	word of mouth

手稿手抄本 handwritten copies of manuscripts
容易出错 be liable to error
石碑摹拓 stone-tablet rubbing
儒家经典 Confucian classics
佛经 Buddhist sutras
木版印刷,雕版印刷 block printing
耗时的;旷日持久的 time-consuming
木块,木板 wooden blocks
雕刻字 engraved words
用墨在纸板/纸上印刷 print with ink on a board/paper
木板 wooden boards
一次使用后变得无用 become useless after one usage
雕;刻 carve
单字 individual characters
印刷文字;字体 types
小陶瓷块 small ceramic blocks
细粘土片 fine clay pieces
湿粘土 moistened clay
(用火)硬化 harden (by fire)
革命性的印刷方法 a revolutionary printing method
知识传播 dissemination of knowledge

Vocabulary

1. alchemy / ˈælkəmi / *n*. 炼金术
2. elixir / ɪˈlɪksər / *n*. 灵丹妙药;炼金药;长生不老药
3. inadvertently / ˌɪnədˈvɜːrtntli / *adv*. 无意地,不经意地
4. sulphur /ˈsʌlfə/ *n*. 硫磺,硫
5. saltpeter / ˌsɔːltˈpiːtə/ *n*. 硝石;硝酸钾
6. charcoal /ˈtʃɑːrkəʊl / *n*. 木炭
7. ore /ɔː(r)/ *n*. 矿石;非金属矿物
8. induce /ɪnˈduːs / *v*. 引起,导致;诱使

火药 **Gunpowder**

古代术士 ancient necromancers
炼金术士 alchemist
炼金术 the practice of alchemy

永生；来世	eternal life
无意地，不经意地	inadvertently
硫磺、硝石和木炭的混合物	a mixture of sulphur, saltpeter, and charcoal
雄黄(二硫化二砷)	realgar
矿石；非金属矿物	ores
燃料，燃烧剂	fuel
正确的比例	the right proportion
诱发爆炸	induce an explosion
烟火	fireworks
庆祝节日和重要事件	celebrate festivals and important events
爆炸性材料	an explosive material
大炮	cannon(s)
火箭；火焰箭	fire arrow
军事用途	military use
有很强的需求	be in great need (of)
大量生产	mass production

Vocabulary

1. navigational /ˌnævɪˈgeɪʃənl/ *adj*. 航行的；航运的
2. magnetize /ˈmægnətaɪz/ *v*. 磁化，受磁
3. traverse /trəˈvɜːs/ *v*. 横过，穿过
4. magnetite /ˈmægnɪtaɪt/ *n*. 磁铁矿
5. lodestone /ˈləʊdstəʊn/ *n*. 天然磁石

指南针	**Compass**
司南	*si nan*, or south governor
指方向	to point the direction
导航工具	navigational tool
不可或缺的，必需的	indispensable
天然的磁铁矿	a natural magnetite
用磁化的钢制成的小针	a tiny needle made of magnetized steel
通过观看太阳、月亮和北极星位置来辨别方向	read the positions of the sun, moon and pole stars to tell directions
地标	landmarks
参照点	points of reference

方位;(用罗盘)定向,测位	bearing
公开水域;开阔水面	open water
陌生领域;陌生领土	unfamiliar territory
多云或恶劣天气	cloudy or bad weather
天然磁石罗盘	lodestone compass
匙形,勺形	spoon-shaped
木质的盘子	a wooden plate
圆形罗盘	the round compass
在浩瀚的海洋上航行	sail on the vast oceans
穿越新领地	traverse new territory
发现新大陆	the discovery of the New World
帆船	sailing ships
长途探险	long-distance exploration
从世界各地获取更多的技术	acquire more technology from around the world
获得巨大的财富	acquire great wealth
环游世界;周游世界;环球旅行	travel around the world

Vocabulary

1. decimal /ˈdesɪml / *adj*. & *n*. 十进位(的);小数(的)
2. acupuncture /ækjuˈpʌŋktʃə/ *n*. 针灸,针刺疗法
3. meridian / məˈrɪdiən / *n*. 子午线,经线;中医经脉
4. utensil / juːˈtens(ə)l / *n*. (尤指厨房或家用)器具,用具
5. astronomer /əˈstrɒnəmə(r) / *n*. 天文学家
6. tremor /ˈtremə(r) / *n*. 轻微地震,小地震
7. Camellia / kəˈmiːliə / *n*. 山茶;山茶花;山茶属
8. horticulture /ˈhɔːrtɪkʌltʃə/ *n*. 园艺,园艺学
9. grafting / ˈgrɑːftɪŋ / *n*. 嫁接法,移植法
10. cocoon / kəˈkuːn / *n*. 茧,卵袋

其他	**Other Important Inventions**
算盘	the Chinese abacus
(算盘上的)杆	rod
(有孔的)珠子	bead
十进位(的),小数(的)	decimal
加	add, plus
减	subtract, minus

乘	multiply
除	divide
[数]平方根	square root
[数]立方根	cube root
针灸,针刺疗法	acupuncture
中医	TCM (Traditional Chinese Medicine)
子午线,经线;中医经脉	meridian
气的流动	the flow of *chi*
[中医]针灸针	acupuncture needle
筷子	chopsticks
象牙	ivory
竹子	bamboo
金属	metal
餐具	eating utensils
风筝	kites
工匠,技工	artisan
救援信号	rescue signals
飞行的乐趣	fly for fun
麻将	mahjong
一种古老的纸牌游戏	an ancient card game
地震仪	seismograph
验震器	seismoscope
天文学家	astronomer
地震检波器	earthquake detector
轻微地震,小地震	tremor
严重,严重性	severity
豆腐	tofu
豆浆;豆奶	soy milk
茶	tea
悬垂的山茶花	an overhanging Camellia bush
山茶花植物	the Camellia sinensis plant
药用	medicinal purpose
园艺,园艺学	horticulture
嫁接法;移植法	grafting
耕作;栽培,培育	cultivate
温室	greenhouse
丝,丝绸	silk
蚕,桑蚕	silkworm
茧,卵袋	cocoon
卷出	reel out

丝线	silken thread
备受追捧的奢侈品	a highly sought-after luxury item
桑树;桑葚	mulberry

A3. Speaking Activities

Situational Speech

Suppose you are an international student studying in an overseas university. You are invited to deliver a speech on class, introducing briefly **the great inventions in ancient China** to your classmates. Prepare a speech of about 5 minutes. Your speech might cover:

- What are the great inventions?
- When and how were they invented?
- How have they developed over the years?
- The significance of these inventions to the whole world.

You may refer to the words and expressions in Part A, but don't confine yourself to them.

Brainstorming

Some inventions, first invented in China, are known to the world by the names of their Western inventors or users. For example, Pascal's Triangle. You may refer to Extensive Reading in A5 for more information. **What factors led to the information asymmetry**? Is it caused by lack of cultural exchanges between China and the West? Or by our lack of efforts to spread Chinese culture in the past? **What should we college students do to tell Chinese stories**? Please elaborate on your views.

Read and Share

Read the following paragraphs about **the four new great inventions** and express your views on one of the five topics below. You may surf online for more information.

As everyone knows, the Four Great Chinese Inventions in ancient times (printing, paper making, the compass and gunpowder) were among the most important technological advances at that time. But things have been changing nowadays. The four great new inventions of China in modern times are Alipay, high-speed train, online shopping, and bike-sharing. They are leading a new trend in convenience and efficiency, and are changing the livelihoods of Chinese people.

Although the technologies of these new inventions did not originate in China and were first devised decades ago, China has outpaced other countries in its widespread adoption and adaptation of all of the four technologies. China is demonstrating its prominence in the industrial and technological revolution via these new inventions. Foreign tourists find that these new inventions pervade the country. As you make your travel plans, keep in mind the four things China does better than anywhere else.

(Adapted from *Chinatravel.com*)

Topics for Sharing:

- What is Alipay and why is it so convenient?
- What is so good about China's high-speed rail?
- How has China become the most popular overseas online shopping country in the world?
- How to access a shared bike?
- How have the four new great inventions changed our life?

Discussion

Creativity is all around us. Without creativity, we would not have the telephone, the telegraph, the radio, the television, the MP3 players, the DVD player, the VCR, or any of today's amazing technology. **Explore and discover creativity or inventions that have made your life more convenient and easier**, especially the ones that are **rarely noticed or have been taken for granted by others**. Discuss with your partners. You may refer to online resources for more useful information.

Interpretation

Interpret the paragraphs below into English with the words and expressions you learned in Part A.

Paragraph 1

中国文化历史悠久,其著称于世的古代四大发明,更是反映了古代中国人民的智慧。造纸术作为我国古代科学技术的四大发明之一,最早起源于西汉时期。经过不断的发展和改造,造纸术最先传入与我国毗邻的朝鲜和越南,东汉末年期间,又经由朝鲜传入日本。唐朝时期,造纸术传入阿拉伯,直到 12 世纪中叶,阿拉伯人才将造纸技术传入欧洲。中国古代造纸术的出现,为世界科学、文化和信息的传播提供了极大的便利,也在一定程度上促进了国家政治、经济、文化的发展,具有划时代的重要意义。

Paragraph 2

印刷术的发明同样是人类历史上最伟大的发明之一。木版印刷在唐代已经是一种广泛使用的技术。但是,这种印刷技术既昂贵又费时。直到宋代(公元 1041—1048 年),毕昇发明了活字印刷术,才使得印刷更加快捷方便。文艺复兴时代,这种印刷技术在整个欧洲迅速传播,直到全世界。

Paragraph 3

指南针是一种显示方向的导航仪器。指南针是公元前 2 世纪至公元 1 世纪之间由中国人发明的。它最早用于风水建筑的布局。到公元1000年,导航罗盘已在船只上普遍使用,从此船只有了导航仪。前往中国的阿拉伯商人学到这项技术,并将其带到西方。火药是古代道教炼金术师于约公元1000年发明的,古代人主要将这项发明用于鞭炮,后来才被用于军事用途。

A4. Culture Highlights

Q: *In the History of Flight pavilion at the National Aeronautics and Space Museum in Washington D.C., a plaque is inscribed to the humble Chinese kite. It states, "The earliest aircraft made by man were the kites and missiles of ancient China." Today, you will see people flying kites with children in many Chinese parks. When were kites invented? Were they flying for fun or for any other purposes?*

A: Kites were invented in the early Warring States Period (475-221 BC) by Mozi and Lu Ban, two philosophers who came after the teachings of Confucius. The kites were exclusive to China for many years before the knowledge of how to make and use them advanced. The period saw many attacks from foreign powers, as well as civil unrest. Kites played a role in providing military intelligence for the Chinese forces.

Originally, they were used for military purposes. The first kites were what we today would call prototype kites: they were made of light wood and cloth. They were designed to mimic a bird's natural flight. The first Chinese kites were used for measuring distances, which was useful information for moving large armies across difficult terrain. They were also used to calculate and record wind readings and provided a unique form of communication similar to ship flags at sea.

Chinese kites today are usually for fun, usually representing mythological characters, symbolic creatures, as well as legendary figures. Some have whistles or strings designed to make unique sounds while flying. We can divide them into two categories: large and small kites. In size they can range between 304 meters and 30 centimeters across.

(Adapted from *Chinahighlights.com*.)

Q: *Marco Polo was probably the most renowned Western traveler of China in ancient times. He was considered "the man who brought China to Europe". Why?*

A: Marco Polo (1254-1324) was a Venetian merchant believed to have journeyed across Asia at the height of the Mongol Empire. He first set out at age 17 with his father and uncle, traveling overland along what later became known as the Silk Road. Upon reaching China, Marco Polo entered the court of powerful Mongol ruler Kublai Khan, who dispatched him on trips to help administer the realm. Marco Polo remained abroad for 24 years. Though not the first European to explore China — his father and uncle, among others, had already been there — he became famous for his travels thanks to a popular book he co-authored while languishing in a Genoese prison.

Most of what is known of Marco Polo's travels in China come from his own hand, so the source is not exactly unbiased. However, taken at his word, he ultimately traveled extensively there, eventually becoming an envoy to the Mongol ruler Kublai Khan. In this enhanced capacity, Polo witnessed phenomena all over the empire, including a vast and astonishingly efficient system of communication and roadways. Additionally, Polo became fascinated with the Chinese usage of paper currency, an idea yet to be fully pondered in his native Europe. He visited Kashgar and Hetian, locations celebrated for beautiful jade. He also visited desert grottoes adorned with magnificent Buddhist carvings.

The most significant and enduring things Marco Polo brought back from China were information and inspiration. During his travels in the East, Polo saw many things that were utterly foreign and new to Europeans, and his later account of his travels generated immense interest among his Western contemporaries. Similarly, his adventures summoned other Europeans to invest in exploration.

(Adapted from *history.com.*, *Chinahighlights.com.*, *europeana.eu.* & *reference.com.*)

A5. Extension

Synonym Discrimination

Can you figure out the differences among the words and phrases below?

Group 1: invention / creation / innovation

Group 2: dissemination / publicity / propaganda / advertisement / broadcast

Group 3: shell / cover / crust

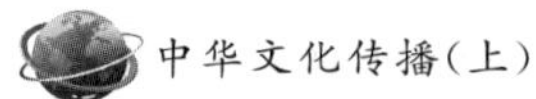

Extensive Reading

Chinese Inventions: What Westerners Might Not Know

China as a nation has the longest and by far the most vast record of inventions in the history of the world. It is now reliably estimated that more than 60% of all the knowledge existing in the world today originated in China, a fact swept under the carpet by the West.

We were all taught in school that the printing press with movable type was invented in Germany by Johannes Gutenberg in about the year 1550. Not so. China not only invented paper but also the printing press with movable set type, which was in common use in China 1,000 years before Gutenberg was born. Similarly, we were taught that Englishman James Watt invented the steam engine. He did not. Steam engines were in widespread use in China 600 years before Watt was born. There are dated ancient texts and drawings to illustrate and prove the Chinese discovered and documented "Pascal's Triangle" 600 years before Pascal copied it, and the Chinese enunciated Newton's First Law of Motion 2,000 years before Newton.

The same is true for thousands of inventions that the West now claim as theirs but where conclusive documentation exists to prove that they originated in China hundreds and sometimes thousands of years before the West copied them.

The Chinese invented the decimal number system, decimal fractions, negative numbers, and the zero, so far in the past that the origin is lost in the mists of time. The Chinese tracked sunspots and comets with such detail and accuracy that these ancient records are still used as the basis for their prediction and observation today. The Chinese were drilling for natural gas about 2,500 years ago, wells 4,800 feet deep, with bamboo pipelines to deliver the gas to nearby cities. The Chinese pioneered the mining and use of coal long before it was known in the West. Marco Polo and Arab traders marveled at the "black stone" that the Chinese mined from the ground, that would burn slowly during an entire night.

China had printed paper money almost 1,500 years ago, done in ways to prevent counterfeiting. Wrapping paper, paper napkins and toilet paper were all in general use in China 2,000 years before the West could produce them. They were the first to invent and develop a full mechanical clock with a true escapement, many centuries before the Swiss had done so. The Chinese invented an ingenious seismograph still in use that tells not only the severity but the direction and distance of earthquakes. The Chinese invented hot-air balloons, the parachute, manned flight with kites, the wheel barrow and matches. They invented hermetically-sealed laboratories for scientific experiments.

They invented belt and chain drives, the paddlewheel steamer, the helicopter rotor and the propeller, the segmental-arch bridge. They invented the use of water power and chain pumps, the crank handle, all the construction methods for suspension bridges, sliding calipers, the fishing reel, image projection, magic lanterns, the gimbal system of suspension. China not only invented spinning wheels, carding machines and looms, but was the world's leader in technical innovations in textile manufacturing, more than 700 years before Britain's 18th century textile revolution.

Chinese expertise with fine porcelain was so advanced millennia ago, that even today it is admitted their ability has never even been equaled in the West, much less surpassed. The Chinese discovered not only magnetism but magnetic remanence and induction, as well as the compass. They invented gunpowder, smoke bombs, the cannon, the crossbow, plated body armor, fireworks, flamethrowers, grenades, land and sea mines, multi-stage rockets, mortars and repeating guns. China had irrigation canals that were also used for transport, and the Chinese invented the canal locks that could raise and lower boats to different levels 1,500 years before the Americans built the Panama Canal. China has earthquake-proof dams functioning today that were built around 250 BC.

A millennium ago, the Chinese conceived and developed the science of immunology — vaccinating people for diseases like smallpox, knowing how to extract and prepare the vaccine so as to immunise and not infect. They discovered the circadian rhythm in the human body, blood circulation and the science of endocrinology. The Chinese were using urine from pregnant women to make sex hormones 2,000 years ago, understanding how they acted on the body and how to use them. Many centuries-old Chinese medical books still exist, documenting all this and much more. Around 1550, China compiled a huge 52-volume Chinese Traditional Herbal Medicine encyclopedia that described almost 2,000 herbal sources and 10,000 medical prescriptions. Among them is chaulmoogra oil, which is still the only known treatment for leprosy.

China designed and built the world's largest commercial ships, which were many times longer and ten times larger in volume than anything the West could build at the time. In the late 1500s the largest English ships displaced 400 tons, while China's displaced more than 3,000 tons. Western ships were small, uncontrollable and fragile, and useless for travelling any distance. Thousands of years ago, Chinese ships had watertight compartments that permitted them to continue journeys even when damaged.

Moreover, Chinese ships not only had multiple masts, but China invented the luff sails which permit us to sail almost into the wind, just as sailboats do today, and were therefore not dependent on wind direction for their travel. Their luff sails contained sewn-in bamboo battens that keep the sails full and aerodynamically efficient, as racing sailboats use today. The Chinese invented the ship's rudder — something the Europeans never managed to do, able to steer themselves only with oars, and European sails permitted them to travel only in the direction of the wind, which meant a ship would have to remain in place, sometimes for months, awaiting a favorable wind.

Chinese maps were the best in the world, by orders of magnitude, for more than a millennium, and the precision of their maps became legendary, being far in advance of the West. The Chinese invented Mercator projections, relief maps, quantitative cartography and grid layouts. China had compasses and such extensive astronomical knowledge that they always knew where they were, could plot courses and follow them by both compass and star charts, and could sail wherever they wanted, regardless of the wind direction. As Needham pointed out, China was so far ahead of the Western world in sailing and navigation that comparisons are just embarrassing. It was only when the West managed to copy and steal China's sailing and navigation technology that it was able to begin travelling the world and colonising it. James Petras wrote, "It is especially important to emphasize how China, the world technological power between 1100 and 1800, made the West's emergence possible. It was only by borrowing and assimilating Chinese innovations that the West was able to make the transition to modern capitalist and imperialist economies."

China was 1,000 years ahead of the West in anything to do with metals — cast iron, wrought iron, steel, carbon steel, tempered steel, welded steel. The Chinese were so skilled at metallurgy they could cast tuned bells that could produce any tone. Long before 1,000 AD, China was the world's major steel producer. I believe it was James Petras who noted that in about 1,000 AD. China was producing about 125,000 tons of steel per year, while 800 years later Britain could produce only 75,000 tons. The Chinese invented the blast furnace, the double-action bellows to achieve the necessary high temperatures for smelting and annealing metals. They invented the manufacture of steel from cast iron. Thy excelled in creating metallic alloys, and very early were casting and forging coins made from copper, nickel and zinc. The entire process of mining, smelting and purifying zinc, originated in China. The Chinese developed the processes of mining itself, and the concentration and extraction of metals.

China was highly advanced in agriculture, having invented the winnowing fan and the seed drill, making an easy process of tilling, planting, and harvesting. Europeans and Americans were still seeding crops by scattering grain from a bag, a greatly wasteful practice that necessitated saving 50% of each year's crop for seed. China developed scientifically efficient plows that have never been equaled and are still used all over the world today. They invented and developed animal harnesses and collars that first permitted horses to actually be used to pull loads. Europe had no efficient plow, and their only way of harnessing animals was to put a rope around their necks, which succeeded only in the animals strangling themselves. The Chinese invented saddles and the riding stirrup. China's food production was orders of magnitude ahead of the world for more than 1,000 years, its advances in agriculture the enabling cause of Europe's agricultural revolution that first permitted it to begin feeding itself adequately. The Chinese were wearing fine silk and cotton clothing and using toilet paper while centuries later Europeans were still wearing animal skins.

Few people in the West are familiar with China's Armillary Spheres. These wonders of the world, cast in bronze several meters in diameter and beautifully decorated with dragons and phoenixes, are some of the oldest and most accurate astronomical observatory instruments in existence, some created more than 3,500 years ago when the Western countries had no knowledge of such things. They determine and measure the positions and equatorial ecliptic and horizontal coordinates of celestial bodies, the positions and daily motions of 1,500 stars and constellations, and much more. When the Western Forces invaded China in the late 1800s, they were so captivated that they plundered most of these treasures and the centuries of data from the ancient observatories, disassembling the instruments and removing them to Europe, returning some to China as part of the Treaties after the First World War.

It leaves one speechless to learn the vast extent of Chinese inventions that existed hundreds of years and often millennia, before they appeared in the West. This isn't simple a matter of gunpowder and fireworks, but of discovery that encompasses the entire range of human knowledge. The inventions are conclusive evidence of Chinese creativity and innovation which can never be erased from the world's historical memory.

(Adapted from *unz.com*)

A6. Assignment

Group Discussion

Form groups of 3 or 4 and discuss "**What is the most important element for a creative mind**?" You may follow the steps below:

- Each one of you write down five elements that you consider essential for a creative mind.
- Delete the one that you consider is less important.
- Repeat the process until there is only one element left on the page.
- Explain to your partners why this element is the most important and see if you could reach an agreement.
- Summarize your group discussion and report to the whole class.

Part B Communication

B1. Introduction

The Silk Road & Zheng He's Voyages to the Western Seas

Over a history of 5,000 years, the Chinese people have always kept an open heart towards friends and cultures from other lands. The silk road, appeared as early as the second century, functioned not only as a trade route, but also a bridge that linked the ancient civilizations of China, India, the Mesopotamian plains, Egypt and Greece. The open and inclusive attitude toward foreign cultures of the Tang Dynasty (618-907) enabled its capital Chang'an to develop into the most prosperous international metropolis in the world of the time. In the Ming Dynasty (1368-1644), Emperor Yongle sent envoys to the Western Seas on seven long voyages. They reached as far as Mecca in West Asia and Mozambique in Africa.

The Silk Road

For more than 1,500 years, the network of routes known as the Silk Road contributed to the exchange of goods and ideas among diverse cultures.

The Silk Road is neither an actual road nor a single route. The term refers to a network of routes used by traders for more than 1,500 years, from when the Han Dynasty of China opened trade in 130 BC until 1453 when the Ottoman Empire closed off trade with the West. German geographer and traveler Ferdinand von Richthofen first used the term "silk road" in 1877 to describe the well-traveled pathway of goods between Europe and East Asia. The term also serves as a metaphor for the exchange of goods and ideas between diverse cultures. Although the trade network is commonly referred to as the Silk Road, some historians favor the term Silk Routes because it better reflects the many paths taken by traders.

The Silk Road extended approximately 6,437 kilometers (4,000 miles) across some of the world's most formidable landscapes, including the Gobi Desert and the Pamir Mountains. With no one government to provide upkeep, the roads were typically in poor condition. Robbers were common. To protect themselves, traders joined together in caravans with camels or other pack animals. Over time, large inns called caravan serais cropped up to house travelling merchants. Few people traveled the entire route, giving rise to a host of middlemen and trading posts along the way.

An abundance of goods traveled along the Silk Road. Merchants carried silk from China to Europe, where it dressed royalty and wealthy patrons. Other favorite commodities from Asia included jade and other precious stones, porcelain, tea and spices. In exchange, horses, glassware, textiles and manufactured goods traveled eastward.

One of the most famous travelers of the Silk Road was Marco Polo (1254-1324). Born into a family of wealthy merchants in Venice, Italy, Marco traveled with his father to China (then Cathay) when he was just 17 years of age. They traveled for over three years before arriving at Kublai Khan's palace at Xanadu in 1275. Marco stayed on at Khan's court and was sent on missions to parts of Asia never before visited by Europeans. Upon his return, Marco Polo wrote about his adventures, making him — and the routes he traveled — famous.

It is hard to overstate the importance of the Silk Road on history. Religion and ideas spread along the Silk Road just as fluidly as goods. Towns along the route grew into multicultural cities. The exchange of information gave rise to new technologies and innovations that would change the world. The horses introduced to China contributed to the might of the Mongol Empire, while gunpowder from China changed the very nature of war in Europe and beyond. The Age of Exploration gave rise to faster routes between the East and West, but parts of the Silk Road continued to be critical pathways among varied cultures. Today, parts of the Silk Road are listed on UNESCO's World Heritage List.

Zheng He's seven voyages to the Western seas

Zheng He left on his 1st voyage in 1405 with a fleet of 240 ships and visited over 30 states along the coasts of the West Atlantic and Indian Oceans. His visits helped to strengthen relations between China and countries in Southeast Asia and East Africa. Zheng's 7th voyage was cut short in 1433 owing to his death at Guli in India. He and his crewmen had traveled as far as the Red Sea and the East African coast.

The first voyage

On June 15th, 1405, Zheng He set sail from Longjiang Harbor in Nanjing, and returned on September 2nd, 1407. According to records, more than 27,800 crewmen participated in the voyage. During this first voyage, Zheng visited Champa (presently Vietnam), Java Island, Malacca, Aru, Samudera, Qiulon, Kollam, Cochin (presently South West India) and Calicut (presently South India).

The second voyage

On September 13th, 1407, only 11 days after his return from the first voyage, Zheng left with his fleet for a second time. During this trip he visited Champa, Java Island, Siam (presently Thailand), Malacca, Cochin, Ceylon (presently Sri Lanka) and Calicut. In July 1409, on his return voyage, Zheng made a special trip to Ceylon and erected a monument at Mt. Ceylon Temple to commemorate the voyage. It was estimated that over 27,000 crewmen had joined in the voyage.

The third voyage

In September 1409, Zheng left with a fleet of 48 ships from Liujiagang, Suzhou in Jiangsu Province, on a third voyage to the West. This time he visited Champa, Java, Malacca, Semudera, Ceylon, Quilon, Cochin, Calicut, Siam, Lambri and Kayal (namely, present-day Vietnam), Indonesia, Malaysia and India. On July 9th, 1411, Zheng was presented with relics from the Buddha via Ceylon, while on his way home.

The fourth voyage

Over 27,670 crewmen were enrolled on Zheng He's fourth journey to the West, which departed in November 1413. They made a detour round the Arabian Peninsula and sailed as far as Mogadishu and Malindi (presently in Kenya). On July 8th, 1415, Zheng and his fleet returned home. At that time, an envoy from Malindi presented giraffes to the Ming emperor.

The fifth voyage

Zheng's fifth voyage to the West started at Quanzhou (presently in Guangdong Province) in May 1417 and ended at Ma Lam (an ancient kingdom in an East African country) via Champa and Java Island. Zheng sailed home on July 17th, 1419. On his return, the Aden Kingdom presented unicorns, Maldive lions and Barawa ostriches to the Ming emperor.

The sixth voyage

On September 30th, 1421, Zheng left China with a fleet of ships to escort foreign envoys home. He passed through Champa, Bengal, Ceylon, Calicut, Cochin, Maldives, Hormuz, Djofar, Aden, Mogadishu and Brava. The fleet returned home on August 18th, 1422, with more envoys from Siam, Samudera and Aden.

In the 22nd year of the Yongle period (1426), the Yongle Emperor passed away, and Zhu Gaozhi (later known as the Renzong Emperor) ascended the throne. Zhu stopped Zheng's voyages to the West, owing to bankruptcy.

The seventh voyage

On December 6th, 1431, Zheng He set sail towards the West for a 7th time, from Longjiangguan (presently Xiaguan in Nanjing, Jiangsu Province). He died from overwork in 1433, on the homeward voyage. The fleet was then led by another eunuch, Wang Jinghong, and returned to Nanjing on July 7th, 1433. The number of crewmen on that voyage was 27,550.

Zheng He's travels to the West were unprecedented in their scale and scope. Zheng made a great contribution to friendly relations between China and the rest of the world in the spheres of politics, economy and culture.

Zheng's travels to the West turned a new page in the history of world marine

navigation, 87 years before Christopher Columbus discovered America, 92 years before Vasco da Gama discovered the Cape of Good Hope and 114 years before Magellan sailed around the globe. In China, Zheng He is regarded as an outstanding diplomat and navigator. His travels to the West made a great impact on world history, for which he is justifiably renowned.

(Adapted from *nationalgeographic.com*. & *Chinahighlights.com*)

B2. Words and Expressions

Vocabulary

1. overland / ˈəʊvəlænd / *adj*. 陆上的;经由陆路的
2. maritime / ˈmærɪtaɪm / *adj*. 海上的,海事的
3. merchandise / ˈmɜːtʃəndaɪs / *n*. 商品,货品
4. caravan / ˈkærəvæn / *n*. 有篷马车;车队,商队
5. boycott / ˈbɔɪkɒt / *v*. 抵制;拒绝参加
6. emissary / ˈemɪsəri / *n*. 使者;密使,特使

丝绸之路	**The Silk Road**
贸易路线网	a network of trade routes
连接东西方	connect the East and the West
陆路;陆地路线	overland routes
海路;海上航线	maritime routes
海洋的	marine
中继贸易	relay trade
商人	merchant
商品	merchandise
最终买家	final buyer
运输货物	transport goods
商队	caravan
塔克拉玛干沙漠	the Taklamakan Desert
绿洲城镇	oasis city
货币经纪人	currency brokers
汇率	exchange rate
奥斯曼帝国	the Ottoman Empire
抵制贸易	boycott trade
使者;密使,特使	emissary

游牧民族,游牧部落	nomadic tribes
远征,考察	expedition
骑兵	cavalry
最受欢迎的商品	the most sought-after commodity

Vocabulary

1. grotto / ˈɡrɒtəʊ / *n*. (人工)洞穴;(屋内的)洞室
2. Mediterranean / ˌmedɪtəˈreɪniən / *adj*. 地中海的
3. mesopotamian / ˌmesəpəˈteɪmiən / *adj*. 美索不达米亚的

丝绸之路沿线地名	**Places along the Silk Road**
中亚	Central Asia
非洲	Africa
欧洲	Europe
天山走廊	Tianshan Corridor
喀什(中国新疆西部城市)	Kashgar
敦煌莫高窟	the Mogao Buddhist Grottoes in Dunhuang
蒙古西部	Western Mongolia
吉尔吉斯斯坦	Kyrgyzstan
塔吉克斯坦	Tajikistan
乌兹别克斯坦	Uzbekistan
土库曼斯坦	Turkmenistan
哈萨克斯坦	Kazakhstan
伊拉克	Iraq
伊朗	Iran
美索不达米亚北部地区	the northern Mesopotamian region
波斯(西南亚国家,现称伊朗)	Persia
以色列	Israel
阿塞拜疆	Azerbaijan
土耳其	Turkey
伊斯坦布尔(土耳其城市)	Istanbul
南高加索	South Caucasus
俄罗斯	Russia
莫斯科	Moscow
阿富汗	Afghanistan
亚美尼亚	Armenia

文莱达鲁萨兰国	Brunei Darussalam
柬埔寨	Cambodia
埃及	Egypt
印度尼西亚	Indonesia
印度	India
马来西亚	Malaysia
莫桑比克	Mozambique
尼泊尔	Nepal
阿曼	Oman
朝鲜	North Korea
韩国	South Korea
朝鲜半岛	Korean Peninsula
葡萄牙	Portugal
巴基斯坦	Pakistan
沙特阿拉伯	Saudi Arabia
斯里兰卡	Sri Lanka
坦桑尼亚	Tanzania
越南	Vietnam
希腊	Greece
意大利	Italy
地中海	Mediterranean Sea

Vocabulary

1. exotic / ɪɡˈzɒtɪk / *adj*. 外来的，异国风情的
2. ornate / ɔːˈneɪt / *adj*. 华丽的，装饰的
3. lacquerware / ˈlækəˌweə / *n*. 漆器
4. tapestry / ˈtæpəstri / *n*. 织锦；挂毯；绣帷
5. cloisonné / klwaːzɒŋˈneɪ / *n*. 景泰蓝

运送物品	**Goods Transported along the Silk Road**
丝绸	silk
瓷器	porcelain
羊毛制品	woolen products
羊毛衣服	woolen clothes
地毯	carpet
窗帘	curtain

毯子,毛毯	blanket
小地毯,毛毯	rug
帕提亚挂毯	Parthian tapestries
地毯编织	carpet weaving
葡萄籽	grape seeds
葡萄树;葡萄藤	grapevine
葡萄酒	grape wine
异国蔬菜和水果	exotic vegetable and fruit
豆角	string beans
芝麻;芝麻籽	sesame seeds
洋葱	onion
胡萝卜	carrot
菠菜	spinach
茄子	eggplant
黄瓜	cucumber
石榴	pomegranate
西瓜	watermelon
香味料,调味料	spices
香水;香料	perfumes
丁香	clove
麝香	musk
玻璃器皿	glassware
檀香,白檀;檀香木	sandalwood
藏红花	saffron
开心果	pistachio nuts
枣子	dates
没药(热带树脂,可作香料、药材)	myrrh
乳香	frankincense
创意和发明	ideas and inventions
道教;道家学说	Taoism
儒家思想;孔子学说	Confucianism
佛教	Buddhism
伊斯兰教	Islam
基督教	Christianity
丝绸面料制作	silk fabric making
造纸术	papermaking techniques
玻璃制造技术	glass making technology
色彩斑斓的景泰蓝	colorful cloisonné
华丽的青铜镜	ornate bronze mirrors
漆器	lacquerware

药物	medicines
金银器皿	gold and silverware
宝石和珠宝	precious stones and jewels

Vocabulary

1. unveil / ˌʌnˈveɪl / *v.* 首次公开，揭幕
2. initiative /ɪˈnɪʃətɪv / *n.* 措施，倡议
3. infrastructure / ˈɪnfrəstrʌktʃə(r) / *n.* 基础设施，基础建设
4. accelerate / əkˈseləreɪt / *v.* (使)加快，促进
5. Eurasia / jʊˈreɪʒə / *n.* 欧亚大陆

一带一路倡议	**Belt and Road Initiative (BRI)**
发展战略	development strategies
(首次)公开；揭幕	unveil
丝绸之路经济带和 21 世纪海上丝绸之路倡议	the Silk Road Economic Belt and 21st-century Maritime Silk Road initiative
欧亚合作	Eurasian cooperation
陆上基础设施走廊	overland infrastructure corridors
海上走廊	sea route corridors
抗衡	counter-balance
多国的，多边的	multilateral
多分支的	multi-branched
基础设施缺口	an infrastructure gap
促进经济增长	accelerate economic growth
涉及 50 多个不同的欧亚国家	involve over 50 different Eurasian countries
促进文化交流	promote cultural exchange
扩大贸易	broaden trade
亚投行，亚洲基建投资银行	Asian Infrastructure Investment Bank
中蒙俄经济走廊	the China-Mongolia-Russia Corridor
欧亚大陆桥	the Eurasian Land Bridge
中巴经济走廊	the China-Pakistan Corridor
中国-中亚-西亚经济走廊	the China-Central Asia-West Asia Corridor
中国-中南半岛经济走廊	the China-Indochina Peninsula Corridor
孟中印缅经济走廊	the Bangladesh-China-India-Myanmar (BCIM) Corridor
冰上丝绸之路	the Ice Silk Road

Vocabulary

1. pilgrimage / ˈpɪlgrɪmɪdʒ / *n*. 朝拜,朝觐;旅行,拜谒
2. expeditionary / ˌekspəˈdɪʃənri / *adj*. 远征的,探险的
3. detour / ˈdiːtʊə(r) / *n*. 绕行,绕道
4. justifiably / ˈdʒʌstɪfaɪəbli / *adv*. 言之有理地,无可非议地
5. relic /ˈrelɪk / *n*. 遗物,遗迹,遗风;圣物,圣骨

郑和下西洋	**Zheng He's Voyages**
海洋探险家	marine explorer
舰队	fleet
一个富有冒险精神的穆斯林家庭	an adventurous Muslim family
前往麦加朝圣	make a pilgrimage to Mecca
虔诚的宗教信仰	pious religious beliefs
七次远征远洋航行	seven expeditionary ocean voyages
中国海洋航行史上的一大壮举	a great feat in the history of Chinese marine navigation
授予某人头衔	confer a title (on sb.)
造船业	the shipbuilding industry
使远距离海洋勘探成为可能	make long-distance oceanic exploration possible
炫耀海洋实力	show off marine prowess
拥有世界上最强大的军队和最大的舰队	boast the strongest army and largest fleet in the world
为海洋勘探奠定良好的经济和军事基础	lay a good foundation economically and militarily for marine exploration
船员	crewmen
扬帆起航	set sail
竖立纪念碑以纪念航行	erect a monument to commemorate the voyage
进行一次特殊的旅行	make a special trip
绕道阿拉伯半岛	make a detour round the Arabian Peninsula
佛陀遗物	relics from the Buddha
长颈鹿	giraffe
独角兽	unicorn
马尔代夫的狮子	Maldive lion
布拉瓦鸵鸟	Barawa ostrich

护送外国使节回国	escort foreign envoys home
规模和范围都是前所未有的	be unprecedented in scale and scope
在世界航海史上翻开新的一页	turn a new page in the history of world marine navigation
为促进中国同世界各国的友好关系作出巨大贡献	make a great contribution to friendly relations between China and the rest of the world
比哥伦布发现美洲早 87 年	87 years before Christopher Columbus discovered America
比达伽马发现好望角早 92 年	92 years before Vasco da Gama discovered the Cape of Good Hope
比麦哲伦环球航行早 114 年	114 years before Magellan sailed around the globe
杰出的外交家和航海家	an outstanding diplomat and navigator
理所当然地出名,无可非议地著名	be justifiably renowned

Vocabulary
peninsula / pəˈnɪnsjələ / *n.* 半岛

郑和下西洋到达国家和地区	**Countries and Places Reached during the 7 Voyages**
占城(印度支那古国,现越南)	Champa (presently Vietnam)
爪哇岛	Java Island
马六甲,马六甲海峡	Malacca
阿鲁,阿鲁群岛	Aru
奎隆(印度喀拉拉邦南部濒阿拉伯海的港口城市)	Kollam (Qiulon)
科钦(现为西南印度)	Cochin (presently South West India)
卡利卡特(现为南印度)	Calicut (presently South India)
暹罗(现泰国)	Siam (presently Thailand)
锡兰(现斯里兰卡)	Ceylon (presently Sri Lanka)
兰布里和卡亚尔(现越南)	Lambri and Kayal (presently Vietnam)
阿拉伯半岛	the Arabian Peninsula
摩加迪沙和马林迪(目前在肯尼亚)	Mogadishu and Malindi (presently in Kenya)
霍尔木兹海峡(在伊朗和阿拉伯半岛之间)	Hormuz
佐法尔(阿曼南部一地区)	Djofar

亚丁(也门人民共和国首都);亚丁湾	Aden
摩加迪休(索马里首都)	Mogadishu
布拉瓦(索马里南部城镇)	Brava

B3. Speaking Activities

Situational Speech

The International Students Association of XXX University is about to hold a seminar on Chinese culture. You are invited to deliver a speech on the seminar, introducing briefly **the Silk Road** to international students. Prepare a speech of about 5 minutes. Your speech might cover:

- History of the Silk Road.
- Countries and regions along the Silk Road.
- Varieties of goods transported along the Silk Road.
- The significance of the Silk Road to the communication between China and other countries in the world.

You may refer to the words and expressions in Part B, but don't confine yourself to them.

Role Play

Imagine yourself as a professor specializing in ancient Chinese history from a world-famous university. You are invited to deliver a lecture on Zheng He's voyages to the West to a class of non-history majors. Your lecture might cover the following topics:

- What are the preconditions of the marine voyages of Zheng He?
- What difficulties did he and his fleet encounter?
- What countries or places did Zheng He visit in the seven voyages respectively?
- What is Zheng He's contribution to global ocean exploration?

Brainstorming

The Analects (*Lunyu*) begins with an edict of Confucius: "How happy we are to have friends from afar?" This shows that the Chinese have always highly respected friends from a long way off and aspired to learn from them. At the same time, the Chinese have always wished to present a good image to outsiders. The open and inclusive spirit of Chinese culture as advocated by Confucius is best exemplified in the prosperity of Chinese economy in recent years. Since the implementation of reform and opening-up policies, the Chinese government has highlighted the importance of openness and inclusiveness. **Why are communication and exchanges critical to the all-round development of a country**? **In what aspects has China's opening-up policy contributed to the development of the whole world**? Please elaborate on your views.

Read and Tell

Read the following paragraphs about **the Belt and Road Initiative** and tell Chinese stories.

Significant progress has been made since the Belt and Road Initiative was first announced in 2013. In Africa, the initiative has provided some of the development tonic many nations sorely need. There have also been notable accomplishments, particularly in Africa, South and Southeast Asia.

In Africa, Belt and Road has provided some of the development tonic many nations sorely need. According to the International Monetary Fund, BRI funding is filling many of the continent's long-standing infrastructure gaps and generating positive ancillary benefits.

The China-Pakistan economic corridor is one of the salient components of BRI to date. This network of projects, together forming the single-biggest BRI programme with financing and infrastructure worth more than USD 60 billion, connects western China to Gwadar — a previously undeveloped, deep-water port on Pakistan's Arabian coast. The corridor will provide a new trading route, opening up the country to multiple industrial and trading opportunities.

(Adapted from *sc.com*)

Ideas for Telling:

- What is the Belt and Road Initiative?
- When was it first announced? Why?
- In what way(s) will the initiative benefit countries around the world?

Interpretation

Interpret the paragraphs below into English with the words and expressions you learned in Part B.

Paragraph 1

丝绸之路是古代连接中西方的商道，一般指陆上丝绸之路。它是汉武帝派张骞出使西域开辟的以首都长安（今西安）为起点，连接地中海各国的陆上通道。传统的丝绸之路，途经中亚国家、阿富汗、伊朗、伊拉克、叙利亚等而达地中海，以罗马为终点，全长6440公里。这条路被认为是连结亚欧大陆的古代东西方文明的交汇之路，而丝绸则是最具代表性的货物。数千年来，游牧民族或部落、商人、教徒、外交家、士兵和学术考察者沿着丝绸之路四处活动。

Paragraph 2

海上丝绸之路形成于汉武帝时代。从中国出发,向西航行的南海航线,是海上丝绸之路的主线。与此同时,还有一条由中国向东到达朝鲜半岛和日本列岛的东海航线,它在海上丝绸之路中占次要的地位。宋代以后,随着中国南方的进一步开发和经济重心的南移,从广州、泉州、杭州等地出发的海上航路日益发达,越走越远,从南洋到阿拉伯海,甚至远达非洲东海岸,人们把这些海上贸易往来的各条航线通称为"海上丝绸之路"。

Paragraph 3

郑和下西洋是明代永乐、宣德年间,郑和担任正使先后七次率领船队进行的海上远航活动。造船业的发达、罗盘的使用、航海经验的积累、大批航海水手的养成、航海知识的增加,为郑和下西洋提供了必要条件。郑和率领船队最远到达东非、红海,加深了大明王朝在海外的影响。郑和下西洋是中国古代规模最大、船只和海员最多、时间最久的海上航行,也是15世纪末欧洲的地理大发现的航行以前世界历史上规模最大的一系列海上探险。

B4. Culture Highlights

Q: *Some scholars say that much of the famous Tang cultural diversity and prosperity had its roots in Silk Road trade exchanges. Why?*

A: During the Tang Dynasty, the Silk Road, which had existed since the Han Dynasty, was reopened and revitalized. It prospered in part because of Tang era territorial expansion which gave the Tang rulers control over crucial parts of Central Asia. Over the Silk Road flowed not just silk, but also an enormous number of other products, people and ideas. So, it is no exaggeration to say that much of the famous Tang cultural diversity had its roots in Silk Road trade exchanges.

The Tang economy also benefited from the existence of strong maritime trade routes. Chinese traders were active in far-flung places like the Persian Gulf, the Arabian Peninsula and Africa. China was already manufacturing a huge range of goods for export by this time, and foreign demand for them drew traders from around the world.

Robust trade links with other regions of the world helped infuse Tang art with many new ideas. The popularity of Buddhism led to the creation of many elaborate works of Buddhist art while improved printing techniques and an increased emphasis on education led to an impressive outpouring of literature and poetry. The Tang Dynasty emperors ruled over a prosperous, multiethnic and cosmopolitan empire. Viewed from the 21st century, their tolerance for diversity seems surprisingly modern.

The Tang capital Chang'an (present-day Xi'an), with a population of 2 million people, was the world's largest city. Contemporary port cities like Guangzhou were filled with an impressive mix of people. Arabs, Hindus, Jews, Christians, Bengalis, Khmers, Persians and Malays lived side-by-side, exchanging both goods and ideas.

At its height, the Tang court received tribute from 72 different states, ruling over a vast territory and ushering in a period of Pax Sinica in Asia. Tang culture had a profound influence on neighboring countries like Japan and Korea and contributed to economic growth all across Central Asia.

(Adapted from *studycli.org*)

Q: *What is the maritime Silk Road? How is it different from the traditional Silk Road?*

A: The maritime Silk Road was a conduit for trade and cultural exchange between China's south-eastern coastal areas and foreign countries. Starting from Quanzhou Fujian Province, the maritime Silk Road was the earliest voyage route that was formed in the Qin and Han dynasties, developed from the Three Kingdoms Period to the Sui Dynasty, flourished in the Tang and Song dynasties, and fell into decline in the Ming and Qing dynasties.

Through the maritime Silk Road, silks, china, tea, and brass and iron were the four main categories exported to foreign countries; while spices, flowers and plants and rare treasures for the court were brought to China. Therefore, the maritime Silk Road was also known as "the maritime china road" or "the maritime spices road".

There were two major routes: the East China Sea Silk Route and the South China Sea Silk Route. The former mainly went to Japan and Korea. It dates back to the Zhou Dynasty (1112 BC) when the government sent some Chinese people to Korea to teach its people farming and sericulture, departing from the port of Bohai Bay, Shandong Peninsula. The latter got its name for being centered around the South China Sea, and its starting points at that time were mainly in Guangzhou, Quanzhou and Ningbo.

The maritime Silk Road fell into decline because of the *Haijin* policy of the Qing Dynasty, which was a ban on maritime activities imposed during the Ming and Qing dynasties.

(Adapted from *Chinahighlights.com*.)

Q: *What is the Belt and Road Initiative? Why is it called the new Silk Road?*
A: Belt and Road initiative is a strategic decision created by the people of China to make a connection between Asia and Europe, and Africa. In 2013, Chinese President Xi Jinping announced this new initiative and invited all the neighboring countries to join in this initiative. Belt and Road Initiative, previously known as one belt one road, is basically a strategic initiative taken by China to build strong connections between Asia and other continents to enhance the international relation of Asian countries with the other countries.
This initiative combines the development of two routes in order to make strong industrial relationships with other countries. The silk route economic belt, a long-term visionary project for the development of infrastructure, connectivity and economy. In this belt, there are six development corridors present to make connections between different countries. The 21st Century Maritime Silk Road connects China to different South-East Asian countries like India, Indonesia, Somalia, Egypt and many more. It also connects the South China Sea, Indian Ocean, Gulf of Bengal and many more.
By December 2021, 145 countries have become part of the Belt and Road Initiative. Not only the Asian countries, some of the Middle East and North African countries also took part in this initiative. The increase in the number of countries joining in this initiative makes its future brighter and more prospective.
(Adapted from *beltroad-initiative.com.* & *unacademy.com.*)

B5. Extension

Synonym Discrimination

Can you figure out the differences among the words and phrases below?

Group 1: road / route / path / pathway / course
Group 2: journey / voyage / trip / expedition /navigation / sail
Group 3: cultivate / plant / rear / foster / nurse / raise

Extensive Reading

Passage One

8 Goods Traded Along the Silk Road

As the name implies, silk was the most representative of the goods traded on the Silk Road. In addition to silk, China's porcelain, tea, paper and bronze products, India's fabrics, spices, semi-precious stones, dyes and ivory, Central Asia's cotton, woolen goods and rice, and Europe's furs, cattle and honey were traded on the Silk Road.

Silk

Chinese silk was sold to Central Asia, Iran, Arabia and the Roman Empire (Europe) along the Silk Road. Silk was the favorite product along the Silk Road. Chinese silk was regarded as a treasure in ancient Central Asia, West Asia, Africa and Europe. The European market had the biggest demand for silk and Chinese silk was highly appreciated in Europe. Colorful silk fabric dazzled the eyes of the people in the vast Roman Empire. The rich and powerful paid huge sums of gold to obtain it. It is estimated that ancient Rome exported as much as 130 tonnes (143 tons) of gold each year to buy silk. Silk was the ideal commodity for silk road trade. Because a caravan's carrying capacity was limited, its products needed to be light and of high value. Silk fitted these characteristics exactly.

Porcelain

China exported porcelain to Japan, the Korean peninsula, Southeast Asia, west and central Asia, east and north Africa and Europe. Porcelain was another product that was prized in the West. The popularity of porcelain even surpassed that of silk in the latter times of Silk Road trade. Silk exports began to decline at the end of the Tang Dynasty (618-907) as silk making techniques spread to central and southern Asia and Europe.

It was during the Han Dynasty era (206 BC-220 AD) that the first kinds of brightly-colored porcelain were manufactured and sent westwards, and especially during the Tang and Yuan (1279-1368 AD) eras, fine porcelain pieces were produced in massive quantities and exported. The 17th and 18th centuries were the golden age of the export of Chinese porcelain. About 200,000 pieces were exported annually in the 17th century. In the 18th century, sales peaked at about a million units a year.

Horses

China initially mainly traded silk for horses from central Asia. Horses were China's most prized import. Horses from central Asia were large and swift — good steads and warhorses. Chinese envoys describe them "winged horses", as they were significantly better than breeds in the empire. China's various dynasties always had a need for horses. Local breeds were considered too small, and they wanted better horses to use in battles against nomads and enemy cavalry. This is actually what spurred the Han court to begin regular Silk Road trade in the 2nd century BC.

Woolen products

Woolens from Central Asia and the eastern Mediterranean were sold to China. Sheep were largely unknown in the eastern empires. Then, woolen clothes, carpets, curtains, blankets and rugs came to China from Central Asia and the eastern Mediterranean. These products impressed the Chinese, because they were unfamiliar with the methods of wool processing, carpet manufacture and weaving. Parthian tapestries and carpets were highly appreciated in the ancient empires.

Food

China received more exotic food than it exported. Tea was the main food export from China. Initially, during the Han era, traders brought in grape seeds. Much of Eurasia had cultivated grapevines and made wines from time immemorial, but the Han, separated from other civilizations by seas, extreme deserts, and high mountains, thought it was novel. They were surprised that people made wine from them.

Other exotic vegetable and fruit imports included:

- String beans from central and south America
- Sesame seeds from ancient central Asia
- Onions from central or west Asia
- Carrots from Persia (now Iran)
- Spinach from Nepal
- Eggplants from India
- Cucumbers from India
- Pomegranates from Persia (now Iran)
- Watermelons from India

Spices and perfumes

The Arabs dominated the spices and perfumes trade. They traded spices to China and Europe. Although it was not the world's only producing area, it monopolized the transshipment trade in India and East Africa — two other sources. By the 10th century, the trade in Europe was almost entirely controlled by Arab traders. China also produced spices, but the variety was very limited due to geographical limitations. Its main spices —cloves and musk — were sold to the West along with silks and porcelain.

Glassware

Glassware was one of the main commodities imported into China from the West. Glassware was novel. It was considered a luxury good in those days. First the Romans and then Samarkand (SE Uzbekistan) made glassware that was especially valued due to its high quality and transparency. Ancient / medieval glassware from west Asia has been unearthed in China, Japan, and Korea.

Slaves

The glorious Silk Road also hosted a dark and tragic slave trade. Slaves were treated as commodities. Many slaves traveled long distances by land and sea to foreign markets far away. Slaves were traded as goods in all the countries along the Silk Road, including Europe, west Asia, Persia, India, Southeast Asia and China. To get slaves across borders, money and animals were paid for a pass. Not only the sellers, but also the local ports, markets and officials benefited. That's why the slave didn't stop until the 19th or 20th century in Asia, long after the Silk Road waned in importance.

(Adapted from *Chinahighlights.com*.)

Passage Two

The Treasure Fleet in Zheng He's Voyages

The vessels needed by the expeditions were constructed at the Longjiang shipyard in the capital by the Yangzi River. The sailors were recruited from coastal provinces, mostly Fujian. During the Ming period, the most popular type of ocean-going ships was the *shachuan*, or "sandboats", with flat-bottom hulls used for travel in the relatively shallow coastal waters. The Fujian shipwrights redesigned the junk for travel in the South China Sea and Indian Ocean. The largest of the junks constituting the fleet, called "treasure ships," had nine staggered masts and twelve sails made of strong silk cloth.

They featured pointed hulls as sharp as knives to cut through large waves, and had high prows and sterns with a keel on the bottom of the hull for enhanced stability in high seas. Wide, overhanging decks were also added: the lowest desk was filled with stones and earth for ballast; the second deck included living quarters for sailors and storage spaces; the third deck contained the kitchen, open space, and the operations bridge; and the fourth deck was a fighting platform, armed with twenty-four cast-bronze cannons. The ships were strengthened by strong prows to ram smaller boats, watertight bulwark compartments for added safety, and a balanced rudder that could be raised and lowered and functioned like an extra keel. These technological innovations were not introduced in Europe until the late eighteenth century.

Rather wide and bulky, the treasure ships were approximately 390-408 feet in length and 160-166 feet in width. With a displacement of 10,000 tons or more, these were undoubtedly the largest wooden sailing ships ever built in world history, dwarfing Columbus's flagship, the St. Maria, which, in contrast, was only 85 feet in length. The actual size of these treasure ships had been controversial, but in 1957, archeologists found in the Longjiang shipyard a huge 36.3-foot-long rudder, a discovery that supported the accuracy of existing records. The reported size of the treasure ships is also consistent with the size of the dry docks at Longjiang, two of them 210 feet wide, big enough to accommodate a ship 166 feet wide.

In addition to the colossal treasure ships, the fleet was composed of other types of specialized vessels of diverse sizes, including the eight-masted "horse ships" that carried horses and building materials needed to repair the fleet at sea, the seven-masted "supply ships" containing food staples for the crew, "troop transports" that accommodated the solders, and fresh water tankers that supplied enough water for continual sailing for one month or longer. The fleet also had two types of warships designed for use against pirates. The ships utilized large flags, signal bells, drums, gongs, lanterns, and carrier pigeons to communicate with one another during the journey.

Eunuchs of different ranks were the top fleet commanders. Fleet crews included military officers, personnel from the Ministry of Rites (in charge of foreign affairs), Ministry of Revenue senior secretaries, astrologers and geomancers, translators knowledgeable of Arabic and other Central Asian languages, and a number of medical officers and pharmacologists whose task was to collect herbs. Regular seamen and soldiers, as well as ironsmiths, caulkers and carpenters to provide needed repairs, constituted the rest of the crew.

(Adapted from *Asianstudies.com*)

B6. Assignment

Poster Design

Suppose an international commodity fair is about to be held in your province. You are invited to design an English poster introducing your local features (e.g., local snack, scenery, history, etc.) to guests from all over the world. You need to

- Consider what local features should be included.
- Design the layout of the local features and words.
- Print and share the poster with your classmates.
- Explain the design process and principle on class.

References

Top 20 Ancient Chinese Inventions. *China Whisper*. Retrieved from https://www.chinawhisper.com/top-20-ancient-chinese-inventions/ on May 1, 2022.

Sally Guo. China's 4 Great New Inventions. *China Travel*. Retrieved from https://www.chinatravel.com/guide/four-great-new-inventions on May 1, 2022.

Chinese Kites — History and Culture. *China Highlights*. Retrieved from https://www.chinahighlights.com/travelguide/culture/kites.htm on May 1, 2022.

What Did Marco Polo Bring Back from China? *Reference*. Retrieved from https://www.reference.com/history/did-marco-polo-bring-back-china-fb192cb0f6b6daf8 on May 1, 2022.

Marco Polo. *History*. Retrieved from https://www.history.com/topics/exploration/marco-polo on May 1, 2022.

Kelly Pang. Walking in the Footsteps of Marco Polo — Discover 13th Century China. *China Highlights*. Retrieved from https://www.chinahighlights.com/travelguide/

article-marco-polo.htm on May 1, 2022.

Beth Daley. Marco Polo — The Man Who Brought China to Europe. *Europeana*. Retrieved from https://www.europeana.eu/en/blog/marco-polo-the-man-who-brought-china-to-europe on May 1, 2022.

Larry Romanoff. History of Chinese Inventions — The Present and The Future — Recent Chinese State of the Art Innovations.*UNZ*. Retrieved from https://www.unz.com/lromanoff/history-of-chinese-inventions-the-present-and-the-future-recent-chinese-state-of-the-art-innovations/ on May 1, 2022.

The Silk Road. *National Geographic*. Retrieved from https://education.nationalgeographic.org/resource/silk-road on May 1, 2022.

Fercility Jiang. Zhen He's Voyages to the West. *China Highlights*. Retrieved from https://www.chinahighlights.com/travelguide/china-history/zheng-he.htm on May 1, 2022.

BRI Projects. Belt and Road Initiative. Retrieved from https://www.beltroad-initiative.com/projects/ on May 1, 2022.

Belt and Road Initiative. *unacademy*. Retrieved from https://unacademy.com/content/karnataka-psc/study-material/international-relations/belt-and-road-initiative/ on May 1, 2022.

Chris Quan. What Was Traded on the Silk Road and Why. *China Highlights*. Retrieved from https://www.chinahighlights.com/silkroad/what-was-traded-and-why.htm on May 1, 2022.

Admiral Zheng He's Voyages to the "West Oceans". *Asian Studies*. Retrieved from https://www.asianstudies.org/publications/eaa/archives/admiral-zheng-hes-voyages-to-the-west-oceans/ on May 1, 2022.

Landmark Achievements of the Belt and Road. *Standard Chartered*. Retrieved from https://www.sc.com/en/feature/landmark-achievements-of-the-belt-and-road/#:~:text on May 1, 2022.

Anne Meredith. The Tang Dynasty: China's Golden Age. *CLI*. Retrieved from https://studycli.org/chinese-history/introduction-to-the-tang-dynasty/ on May 1, 2022.

Kelly Pang. The Maritime Silk Road. *China Highlights*. Retrieved from https://www.chinahighlights.com/travelguide/maritime-silk-road.htm on May 1, 2022.

Unit 4 Traditional Arts

Part A Peking Opera & Chinese Calligraphy

A1. Introduction

Traditional Chinese Art Forms You Need to Know

Traditional art forms offer a fascinating peek into Chinese culture from hundreds, if not thousands of years ago, and are still practiced even in today's hyper-modern China. They are uniquely Chinese, and vastly different from the art styles of the west. Here, as a dedicated fan of Chinese culture, I'd like to take you to two of the major traditional art forms of China: Peking Opera and Chinese calligraphy.

Peking Opera

Peking Opera, also referred to as *Jingju* or *Jingxi* in Chinese, is regarded as the national opera in China and the quintessence of Chinese culture in Chinese minds. It is an art form combining music, vocal performance, mime, dance, and acrobatics. It was declared World Intangible Cultural Heritage of Humanity by the United Nations Educational, Scientific and Cultural Organization (UNESCO) in 2010.

In 1790, Emperor Qianlong of the Qing dynasty summoned opera troupes from different areas around China to perform for him in Beijing in celebration of his 80th birthday. After the celebration, four troupes from Anhui Province were asked to stay, for audiences were particularly satisfied with their beautiful melodies, colorful costumes, and interesting facial patterns. Gradually it replaced Kunqu Opera which had been popular in the palace and among the upper ranks in Beijing. Later, some troupes from Hubei Province came to Beijing and often performed together with the Anhui troupes. The two types of performance blended and gradually gave birth to a new genre that came to be known as Peking Opera.

Peking Opera was originally an exclusively male pursuit. The appearance of women on the stage began unofficially during the 1870s, when female performers began to play male roles and declared equality with men. The characters staged in Peking Opera are not based on the appearance of people in daily life. Artistic exaggerations are applied in elaboration of make-up and costumes according to gender, personality, age, occupation, and social identities of the roles in different plays. The roles generally fall into four categories: *sheng* (male), *dan* (female), *jing* (male, painted-face characters) and *chou* (male, clowns).

Audiences can tell a player's role, occupation and even personality by the color of his robe or the wings on his hat because they all convey different meanings. For example, lower-level officials usually wear orchids or Buddhist knots and only the emperor could wear yellow.

The repertoire of Peking Opera is mainly based on Chinese history, folklore, and contemporary life. Here are some recommended classics of Peking Opera: *The Drunken Concubine* (Gui Fei Zui Jiu), *Farewell My Concubine* (Ba Wang Bie Ji) and *Daiyu Buries Flowers* (Daiyu Zang Hua).

Chinese calligraphy

Calligraphy established itself as one of the major Chinese art forms during the Han dynasty (206 BCE-220 CE), and for two millennia after, all educated men were expected to be proficient at it. Calligraphy is an artistic form that is widely practiced and revered in the Chinese cultural sphere. It aimed to demonstrate superior control and skill with brush and ink.

Far more than mere writing, the art used varying thicknesses of brushstroke, their subtle angles, and their fluid connection to each other — all precisely arranged in imaginary spaces on the page — to create an aesthetically pleasing whole. When practicing calligraphy, one should pay attention to the features and implications of the characters as well as their strokes and components so as to make them an art piece. As a unique performing art, it is often regarded as sheer life experienced through energy in motion that is registered as traces on silk or paper, with time and rhythm in shifting space being its main ingredients. A connoisseurship quickly developed, and calligraphy became one of the six classic and ancient arts alongside ritual, music, archery, charioteering, and numbers.

The essential implements of Chinese calligraphy are brush, ink, paper, and inkstone. The body of the brush can be made from either bamboo, or rarer materials such as red sandalwood, glass, ivory, silver, and gold. Its head can be made from the hair or feathers of a wide variety of animals. Ink and inkstone enjoy a time-honored history too. The use of them can be traced back to over 2,000 thousand years ago. Ink is made from lampblack (soot) and binders, and comes in ink sticks which must be rubbed with water on an ink stone until the right consistency is achieved. Both bamboo and silk had served as the writing materials before paper was widely used.

The styles of Chinese calligraphy refer to the fonts of the characters. Traditionally, there are altogether five types, namely running script, cursive script, regular script, seal script and clerical script. And there are some subcategories subordinate to each style. For instance, seal script can be further divided into two types, namely large seal script and small seal script.

Closing words

Art in China has grown in a phenomenal way, and adapted and changed along with the culture and traditions. Ancient Chinese art is not limited to the above-mentioned ones; rather these examples have partly created a foundation for future artistic accomplishments and served as a bridge through which the traditional Chinese culture is introduced to other parts of the world.

(Adapted from *topchinatravel.com*, *chinaculturetour.com*, *worldhistory.org*)

A2. Words and Expressions

Vocabulary

1. quintessence /kwɪnˈtesəns/ *n.* 精髓,精华;典范,典型
2. vignette /vɪˈnjet/ *n.* (清晰描述特点的)片段,短文;插曲
3. walk-on /ˈwɑːkɑːn / *n.* & *adj.* (戏剧或电影中的)龙套角色;小角色的
4. repertoire /ˈrepətwɑːr/ *n.* 全部剧目,全部节目
5. whisker /ˈwɪskə/ *n.* (尤指男子侧面或下巴上的)胡须,络腮胡
6. percussion /pəˈkʌʃən/ *n.* 打击乐器(钟、鼓、铃、铜钹等);敲打,碰撞
7. prop /prɑːp/ *n.* & *v.* 道具;支撑,支持
8. choreography /ˌkɔːriˈɑːɡrəfi/ *n.* 编舞艺术·舞蹈设计
9. inscribe /ɪnˈskraɪb/ *v.* 雕,刻;题写
10. embody /ɪmˈbɑːdi/ *v.* 体现,表现;包括

京剧	**Peking Opera**
国粹,民族精华	national quintessence
中国文化瑰宝	a gem of the Chinese culture

表演京剧	perform Peking Opera
观看京剧片段	watch a vignette of Peking Opera
剧团	opera troupe
观众	spectator
梨园	the Pear Garden
文戏	civilian play
武戏	military play
唱腔	singing melody
脸谱	painted face / face-painting
生	male role / *sheng*
旦	female role /*dan*
净	painted-face male role /*jing*
丑	male clown role /*chou*
名角，大腕	celebrated performers / big shot
资深戏剧艺术家	veteran dramatic artists
跑龙套	play a walk-on / play an extra
替身演员	stunt double
唱、念、做、打	singing, speaking, acting and fighting
主要使用北京方言	primarily use Beijing dialect
吸收地方戏剧形式	absorb regional dramatic forms
描绘历史故事	depict historical stories
丰富的剧目	abundant repertoires
夸张的妆容	exaggerated facial make-up
灿烂的颜色	resplendent colors
艳丽的服饰	flamboyant costume
长袍和配饰	robes and accessories
人造胡须	artificial whisker
打击乐器	percussion instrument
弦乐器和管乐器	string and wind instrument
舞台布置	stage settings
精心制作的道具	well-crafted props
设定节目的节奏	set the pace of the show
推动故事的发展	propel the progress of the story
营造特别的氛围	create a particular atmosphere
刻画人物的个性	portray characters' personalities
既定的动作编排	established choreography for movements
舞台上的精彩表演	attractive spectacle onstage
赢得观众赞赏的掌声	win admiring applause from the audience
创造一个形象世界	create a world of image
以公式化和象征性为特色	feature a formulaic and symbolic style

采用师傅带徒弟的培训方式	adopt a master-student training mode
历经长期的训练和学徒期	undergo long periods of training and apprenticeship
口头指导、观察和模仿	oral instruction, observation and imitation
感受其内涵和魅力	feel its connotations and allure
培养某人对戏剧的热情	instill the passion for opera in someone
历经岁月的起起落落	experience both highs and lows throughout the ages
推广古典戏剧流派	popularize classic opera genres
海外巡回演出	overseas performance tour
为京剧赢得国际声誉	win an international reputation for Peking Opera
体现中国传统文化精髓	embody the essence of traditional Chinese culture
被列入人类非物质文化遗产代表名单	be inscribed on the Representative List of the Intangible Cultural Heritage of Humanity

Vocabulary

1. stroke /strəʊk/ *n*. (书写或绘画的)笔画,一笔,一画;中风;斜杠;泳姿
2. wield /wiːld/ *v*. 挥舞;抓握(工具或武器);运用权力;施加影响
3. cursive /ˈkɜːsɪv/ *adj*. 草书的;连笔的
4. aesthetic /esˈθetɪk/ *adj*. 审美的,美感的,美学的;艺术的
5. brushwork /ˈbrʌʃwɜːk/ *n*. 笔触,笔法;画法,画风
6. virtuosity /ˌvɜːtʃuˈɑːsəti/ *n*. (表演或演奏方面的)高超技艺,精湛演技
7. sage /seɪdʒ/ *n*.& *adj*. 智者,贤人;(尤指因经验丰富而)睿智的,明智的
8. mount /maʊnt/ *v*. 装裱;安装;开展;登上;上升
9. trace /treɪs/ *v*.& *n*. 临摹,描摹;追溯,跟踪;发现;痕迹
10. gem /dʒem/ *n*. 宝石;难能可贵的人(或物);被人喜爱的人(或物)

书法	**Calligraphy**
汉字	Chinese character
方块象形文字	square-shaped pictographic character
飞舞的笔画	flying stroke
线条的艺术	the art of lines
写书法	practice calligraphy
毛笔	writing brush / ink brush / hair brush

挥笔	wield the brush
柔软而有弹性的	supple and elastic
将它蘸上墨水	dip it in ink
写(画)一笔,做出笔触	make a stroke
横、竖	rightward stroke and downward stroke
点、提	tiny dash and rising
撇、捺	left-falling and right-falling
弯、折	bend and break
钩、斜	hook and slant
书体	calligraphy font
行书	running script
草书	cursive script / drafting script
楷书	regular script
篆书	seal script
隶书	clerical script
硬笔书法	hard-nib calligraphy
软笔书法	soft-nib calligraphy
连笔和简笔	connected and simplified strokes
遵循严格的规则	follow restrictive rules
将字整齐放入方框	place characters neatly into square boxes
创造美观的整体	create an aesthetically pleasing whole
审美标准	aesthetic standard
笔法或画风的高超技艺	virtuosity of the brushwork
独树一帜	form an individual path with one's own style
发明颜体	develop the Yan style
书法大家	master calligrapher
业余书法爱好者	amateur calligrapher
书圣	the Sage of Calligraphy
文房四宝	the Four Treasures of the Study
笔墨纸砚	brush, paper, ink stick and ink slab
华丽的镇纸	ornate paperweight
(刻有姓名或图案的)印章	carved seal / carved block
将它先后在红色印泥和纸上按压	press it into a red paste and onto paper
盖章(并印出图案)	stamp an image
装裱书法作品	mount a calligraphic work
临摹一副手稿	trace a script
真迹,真实的手稿	genuine manuscript
石刻碑文	stone inscription
存世名作	a masterpiece surviving to this day
一气呵成	written at one go

传达难以表达的(情感或事物)	convey the inexpressible
唤起内心的平静	evoke a sense of inner peace
提升某人的气质	refine one's temperament
自我表达的手段	a means of self-expression
情绪的升华	a distillation of mood
在混乱中得到内心解脱	a feeling of release from the turmoil
中华民族的无价之宝	invaluable treasure of the Chinese nation
面临期待已久的复兴	face a long-awaited renaissance
具有鲜明特色的独特艺术形式	unique artistic form with distinctive characteristics
字体之间相互独立。	The characters remain separate from each other.
字体之间相互连接。	The characters run into each other.

Vocabulary

1. lyre /laɪ/ *n*. 里拉琴(琴身为 U 形的古弦乐器)
2. porcelain /ˈpɔːrsəlɪn/ *n*. 瓷;瓷器
3. embroidery /ɪmˈbrɔɪdəi/ *n*. 绣花,刺绣(品);(对故事等的)渲染,修饰
4. clay /kleɪ/ *n*. 黏土;陶土

其他传统艺术形式	**Other Traditional Art Forms**
琴棋书画	lyre-playing, chess, calligraphy and painting
国画	traditional Chinese painting
中国戏曲	Chinese opera
制瓷	porcelain-making
编织工艺	weaving technology
中国结	Chinese knot
刺绣	embroidery
陶艺	pottery
糖画	sugar painting
玉雕	jade carving
根雕	root carving
木偶戏	puppet show
皮影戏	shadow play
剪纸	paper-cutting
泥塑	clay sculpture
杂技	acrobatics

折扇	folding fan
建筑	architecture
雕塑	sculpture
诗歌	poetry
武术	martial arts

A3. Speaking Activities

Invitation Call

Make a phone call to Mr. Johnson, a foreign teacher at your university, inviting him to a cultural exchange activity featuring Peking Opera. In your call, you need to specify the following information and add more details as necessary.

- date and venue
- scheduled activities (a speech on Peking Opera, a live performance, learning face-painting techniques and trying on the opera costumes on the spot, etc.)
- an early reply is appreciated

Brainstorming

Chinese calligraphy is a unique cultural symbol for this ancient country to share with the rest of the world its vast and extensive culture. It appears to be simple with only the combination of dots and strokes, but behind this simple combination, there exists infinite cultural profoundness and richness. What can we do to help preserve and develop traditional cultures like Chinese calligraphy? Please elaborate on your views.

Read and Share

Read the following paragraphs about **how to popularize Peking Opera** and share your views.

Paragraph 1

Peking Opera has been widely acknowledged and propagated as a "gem of the Chinese culture" and an important part of the Chinese national identity. The first artist to introduce Peking Opera abroad was Mei Lanfang, one of the most celebrated Peking Opera performers in China. He brought the art first to Japan in 1919, then to the United States in 1930 and to Europe in 1935. Ever since then the art has become even more popular both at home and abroad. However, most Peking Opera plays are based on Chinese folklore and historical stories which are difficult to understand for people unfamiliar with the Chinese culture. In order to help foreign audiences understand the art better, Mei Lanfang took along with him 183 painted scrolls as well as 1987 drawings with pictures and explanations when he made his first tour in the United States.

(Adapted from *lifeinchinatoday.com*)

Paragraph 2

For some young people, Peking Opera remains a classic art form that stays distant from their life. The art has fallen out of favor with the younger generation as the Internet and other forms of entertainment have emerged. Wang Peiyu, a Peking Opera artist, never hesitates to embrace new media and modern forms of communication, such as online streaming, lectures and variety shows, to promote the art. She adopts the trendy words, catchphrases, and context of the younger generation to introduce Peking Opera to new audiences. "Peking Opera is now in an era where inheritance is as important as popularization, but to some extent, I think the latter is more important now. We should not only cultivate Peking Opera performers; we should also cultivate the fans and spectators. Only when the younger generation loves Peking Opera, will the art truly have vitality," Wang said.

(Adapted from *news.cgtn.com*)

Ideas for Sharing:

- What is the best way to present Peking Opera to foreign audiences?
- What is the best way to promote Peking Opera among college students in China?
- Do you think it appropriate to fuse traditional opera with trending culture?

Debate

Handwriting has been an integral part of human life for thousands of years. They were invented and used to record thoughts and experiences. With the advent of modern technology, handwritten records have gradually lost their importance. Digital communication and the printed words are taking over.

(Adapted from *craft-art.com*)

Topic for Debate:

Is it necessary for young people to learn Chinese calligraphy?

Interpretation

Interpret the paragraphs below into English with the words and expressions you learned in Part A.

Paragraph 1

京剧被称为中国的国粹之一，它将音乐、舞蹈、文学、美术、武术和杂技融于一体，是中华民族传统文化的重要表现形式。京剧拥有丰富的演出剧目、卓越的表演艺术家和大批的忠实观众，对中国及周边国家有着深远影响。2010 年，京剧被列入联合国教科文组织人类非物质文化遗产代表名录。

Paragraph 2

京剧角色主要分为"生""旦""净""丑"四种行当，分别代表男子、女子、性格粗犷豪迈的男子(俗称花脸)和滑稽风趣的小人物。这些角色不是按照生活里的原貌出现的，而是根据其性别、年龄、性格、职业以及社会地位，在妆容、服装、动作等方面加以艺术的夸张，以此来塑造剧中人物。

Paragraph 3

京剧脸谱不同于面具，面具是罩在人脸上的，而脸谱是用不同的颜色在演员脸上勾画出来的。京剧脸谱五彩缤纷，极其夸张而又极其艳丽。每种颜色和图案都有独特的象征意义，观众可据此判断人物的性格和身份。脸谱主要用于"净"和"丑"两种角色，比如，红脸表示忠勇，黑脸表示粗犷，白脸表示奸诈。

Paragraph 4

中国有书法艺术，得力于两个因素。一是汉字，它是一种方块象形文字，具有独特的美感。二是毛笔，它柔软而富有弹性，可以产生变化多端的笔触。书法是线条的艺术。欣赏书法作品时，观者可充分感受到书法家挥毫泼墨、一气呵成的高超技艺。书圣王羲之的存世名作便是最好的典范。

Paragraph 5

书法是一种具有鲜明特色的艺术形式，分为篆书、隶书、楷书、行书和草书五种书体。它的书写需遵循严格的规则，以创造整体的美感为目的。同时，书法还需借助一整套工具来完成，人们称之为"文房四宝"，即"笔墨纸砚"。很多书法爱好者通过临摹大师的作品来提升自己的书艺和气质。

A4. Culture Highlights

Q: *Mask brings infinite imagination to people. What comes to your mind when you think of mask? Is it an Egyptian pharaoh's mask, a Venetian carnival mask, the theatrical mask of Chinese opera, or the phantom of Western art?*

A: The first thing coming to my mind is the **face-painting** or **lianpu** of Peking Opera. The key to appreciating and understanding Peking Opera as it depicts scene after scene of ancient stories about noble and brave characters like Zhang Fei and Guan Yu from the Three Kingdoms, fictitious figures like Monkey King from *Journey to the West*, shady figures like Cao Cao and so on, lies in understanding the patterns and colors of the opera's painted faces.

The origin of face-painting can be traced back to the Southern and Northern dynasties (420-581), when leading actors used to wear masks. As the operatic arts developed, performers gradually took off their masks, and painted colorful patterns directly on their faces instead so that audiences could easily identify their facial expressions.

The facial make-up is **marked and erudite**, which **denotes the nature and personality** of the character. Certain colors are used to signify qualities and imperfections. Red is the color of loyalty, integrity, and courage; black suggests a serious and taciturn disposition, including strength and roughness; white reveals a crafty and suspicious character. Gold and silver faces symbolize mysteriousness and stand for monsters or gods.

(Adapted from *news.cgtn.com*)

Q: *Calligraphy is a form of ornamental handwriting found in various cultures throughout the world. What are the similarities and differences between Western calligraphy and Chinese calligraphy?*

A: All types of calligraphy in general originated as hieroglyphics, picture, symbols, etc. Before the **printing press** was invented in both Western and Chinese culture, every single letter or character of every book had to be **hand-drawn**. This led to the formation of many different forms of calligraphy. After the printing press was invented, Western calligraphy sharply declined in popularity. However, it was revived recently and is now considered a hobby that many still enjoy.

Calligraphy is the art of giving form to signs in an expressive, harmonious, and skillful manner. Western calligraphy mostly requires a flat-edged pen to achieve the result while the Chinese use **a pointed but flexible hair brush** to make long and short strokes. Since the writing utensil is different, the outcome varies too. For example, a stroke from a pen was lighter than a stroke from a brush dipped in ink.

Chinese calligraphy differs from **penmanship**, **typography** or **handwriting** as characters are disciplined yet fluid and spontaneous. Often, they are **improvised** at the moment of writing. The artistic manifestation takes precedence over the legibility of the characters. That's why Chinese calligraphy is viewed as a very **high art form** in Asian culture and respected as something much more than a hobby.

(Adapted from *prezi.com*)

A5. Extension

Synonym Discrimination

Can you figure out the differences among the words below?

Group 1: opera / drama / play / musical
Group 2: conserve / preserve / keep / maintain
Group 3: calligraphy / penmanship / typography / handwriting

Extensive Reading

Passage One

A Brief Introduction to Peking Opera

Peking Opera is a colorful, spectacular performance art that dazzles, fascinates, and often puzzles foreigners. A quintessentially Chinese art form, its elaborate costumes and makeup, gestural and acrobatic stage movements, highly symbolic and stylized content, and unique musical style amaze and intrigue audiences. The art might be best thought of as a confluence of stylized patterns of dress, makeup, action, staging, text, and music. Each of these parameters is the fruit of a system several centuries old, presented as living art through the work of highly trained performers. This essay attempts to present an introduction to Peking Opera that provides insight for teachers and students approaching the art while avoiding excess specialized terminology.

Peking Opera (known as *jingju*, or opera of the capital in China) is one of more than three hundred types of traditional Chinese opera, and it is probably the best-known. Four Chinese opera types are now inscribed in the United Nations Educational, Scientific, and Cultural Organization's "Representative List of the Intangible Cultural Heritage of Humanity." Peking Opera was added to this list in 2010.

Many modern Chinese do not enjoy Peking Opera at all; like Western opera, it seems to be both an acquired taste and a genre mostly appreciated by older Chinese. This may simply indicate that a taste for Peking Opera is often developed over several decades of a person's life, as is often the case for the Western operas, such as those written by Giuseppe Verdi, Richard Wagner, and others. Nevertheless, Peking Opera is commonly performed for tourists in China, at festivals for Chinese audiences, and on tours worldwide. It is also disseminated via DVD / video and audio recordings, Chinese television broadcasts, and YouTube, among many Internet sources. It is highly prized by the Chinese in general as an artistic, historically significant, representative art form.

History and context

Peking Opera traditionally features singing actors and actresses wearing magnificent costumes reminiscent of Ming dynasty (1368-1644) dress, although modern operas — those created since 1912, when imperial rule ended — may call for modern dress. The bulk of Peking operas date from imperial times and involve characters from Chinese history, legend, and myth. Peking Opera performances often consist of famous scenes excerpted from several different stories rather than illustrating a single narrative plot. Peking Opera is an amalgam of regional opera types that have been in existence for centuries.

Plays and spoken narratives with music have been performed in Chinese villages, towns, and cities for centuries. In the long history of Chinese opera types, the late eighteenth century was particularly significant, as members of the imperial family began to take an intense interest in these art forms. The year 1790 marked a watershed in the history of the art form. To celebrate the Qianlong emperor's eightieth birthday, several opera troupes came from Anhui Province to perform in Beijing. The shows were highly successful, and the art began to attract patrons and audiences in the capital and evolved traits that eventually distinguished "opera of the capital" from other types. During the final decades of the nineteenth century, the Dowager Empress Cixi (1835-1908) was a notable supporter of Peking Opera. She had special palace opera theatres built to indulge her interest in the art.

Peking Opera continued to attract attention in the decades between the end of imperial rule in 1912 and the founding of the People's Republic of China on October 1, 1949. Four Peking Opera actors became especially famous for their portrayals of women on stage during this era. Of these, Mei Lanfang (1894-1961) was the most famous, eventually performing in Japan, America, and Europe; some of his work was filmed. Mei Lanfang specialized in playing young women and was celebrated for embodying these roles perfectly. His influence in China as well as in the West cannot be overestimated. By the end of his 1935 trip to Russia, Germany, and America, his work had gained the admiration of Western theater luminaries.

Peking Opera roles, costumes, and makeup

There are four main types of roles in Peking Opera: male (*sheng*), painted-face male (*jing*), female (*dan*), and clown (*chou*). Each of these role types has several different subsets differentiated by age and personality. An experienced operagoer recognizes role types immediately because of their association with specific costumes and makeup. Costumes and makeup are stylized rather than life-like. For instance, martial characters often wear a set of four pennants or flags attached to the back of their costumes. Obviously false beards and exaggerated facial makeup function as symbols for communicating the character's status. The male *sheng* characters (subcategorized by age and profession) often have some sort of beard and relatively naturalistic facial coloring, but the painted-face male *jing* roles call for brightly painted facial designs in vivid colors, including red, black, white, blue, and yellow. *Jing* characters are powerful men, sometimes even supernaturally so. The colors used in *jing* makeup have specific connotations. For example, red indicates loyalty and bravery; yellow connotes clever deviousness. Female (*dan*) roles fall into groups such as *qingyi* (young lady), *wudan* (woman warrior), and *laodan* (old woman). The *jing* and *qingyi* roles feature elaborate headdresses and robes. Just as pennants or flags worn on the back indicate a martial role, extremely long white sleeves are worn by upper-status men and women. Skillful manipulation of these "water sleeves" is an art in itself. Clown (*chou*) characters are identified by a patch of white in the center of the face.

Singing style and texts

Peking Opera singers vocalize with a tonal quality that can be characterized as bright, straight, and nasal. These sounds are quite dissimilar from Western operatic vocal production. The singing features long, drawn-out syllables, and rarely does it feature the extremes of held-out high pitches combined with vocal agility highly prized in Western opera. The nature of the Chinese language (which is tonal and features many sounds not found in English or other European languages) contributes significantly to the emphatic rendering of Peking Opera's melodic passages. Because the singing style is much less relaxed and rounded than much Western singing, Peking Opera often sounds harsh to American audiences.

Lyrics for Peking Opera are most often in the form of couplets — groupings of two lines — and fall into two large language categories: *wenyan wen* (classical Chinese) and *baihua* (plain or vernacular language). Because Peking Opera relies heavily on displaying the complexity of these linguistic attributes, it is not surprising that it is doubly difficult for non-Chinese listeners to appreciate it fully. Melodically, Peking Opera utilizes two frameworks: the lively, generally higher *xipi* mode, and the lower, more sedate *erhuang* mode. Each character and scene calls for specific types of lyrics and melodies, just as costumes and makeup are configured from suitable established stylized types.

Instrumental music

Peking Opera features an instrumental music ensemble that functions as an accompaniment to singers' voices and rarely performs as an independent unit. The Peking Opera orchestra typically features fewer than a dozen players who are led by a conductor playing a wooden clapper and a drum. Other than the conductor, who is called on to perform throughout an opera, the instrumentalists generally fall into two groups: civilian, or *wenchang* / string and wind, and martial, *wuchang* / gongs and drums. Essential instruments in the civilian ensemble are the *jing hu*, *erhu* — bowed two-string fiddles, the *jing hu* sounding high pitches and the *erhu* lower — and *yue qin* — the plucked "moon lute" with a round body. In the martial section, the clapper and drum, and two types of gongs plus a pair of cymbals are the most basic instruments. The gongs used in Peking Opera have distinctive tones that rise and fall. The civilian and martial sections of the orchestra play together during most parts of the opera, and additional instruments are commonly heard. These include the *san xian*, *ruan*, and *pipa* (plucked string instruments), *dizi* (horizontal flute), *suona* ("Chinese oboe"), *sheng* (a type of mouth organ), and a variety of drums and gongs. In general, the *jing hu* doubles melodies as they are sung, and other melodic instruments reinforce the line, adding slight rhythmic variations. Percussion instruments punctuate speech and serve as accompaniments to dance and combat scenes as well as undergirding the work of the civilian ensemble.

Scenery, acrobatics, dance, and mime

In terms of scenery, Peking Opera is minimalistic, but in terms of stage action, it is frequently dramatic, energetic, and strenuous. Peking Opera is therefore nearly the opposite of Western opera in terms of scenery and stage action. Western opera usually favors carefully constructed, often massive sets and is notably undemanding of physical action on the part of singers. No matter the venue, Peking Opera scenery is likely to be no more than a carpet, a few chairs, and perhaps a table and cloth. Peking Opera performers and audiences use their imaginations to envision a room suggested only by a table or a few chairs or perhaps a mountainside. Performers usually engage in elaborate acrobatic feats and/or dance during the course of the opera, delighting audiences. Actions involve jumping, whirling, dancing, twirling various sorts of props, climbing and balancing, and somersaults, all demanding a high level of athletic training. Stylized actions occur: short circular walks symbolize events such as long journeys; wriggling fingers denote high emotion. Dancing is often called for by the storyline rather than being extraneous to it. In *The King Bids Farewell to His Favorite Concubine*, the king's favorite concubine performs a dance in order to lift the king's spirits: a climactic moment in the story. Solo as well as ensemble dances are commonly seen. Mimed portions of operas include actions such as sewing, opening and closing doors, and pouring tea, all done in a stylized but recognizable fashion. The ability of the actor to evoke the action is prized, whereas the addition of props or scenery for the purpose of direct illustration would probably seem clumsy and obvious.

Closing words

Peking Opera enthusiasts are likely to number in the hundreds of thousands, if not millions. There are ample reasons to be optimistic about the future of Peking Opera. Children with talent for acting, acrobatics, dancing, and singing in operatic style are certainly not in short supply in China. Interest in fostering the traditional arts is strong, both in China and in diasporic communities, and on certain festive occasions, there seems to be no adequate substitute for a Peking Opera performance. The Chinese government has extended support to training schools, troupes, and theaters. Tourists, both Chinese and from abroad, continue to enjoy the art. Finally, amateur interest and performance groups are alive and functioning in China, and some of these are based at Chinese universities. The fact that UNESCO has inscribed Peking Opera in the "Representative List of the Intangible Cultural Heritage of Humanity" — is indicative of the high value the Chinese accord Peking Opera and its current health, boding well for the future of this unique, distinctively Chinese art form.

(Adapted from *asianstudies.org*)

Passage Two

Chinese Calligraphy

Calligraphy is the world's oldest abstract art — the art of the line. This basic visual element can also hold a symbolic charge. Nowhere has the symbolic power of the line manifested itself more fully than in Chinese calligraphy, a tradition that spans over 3,000 years. The aesthetics of calligraphy are important to the history of art in East Asia, where during much of its premodern era classical Chinese was the lingua franca.

History of Chinese calligraphy

Chinese calligraphy is a unique artistic form of Chinese cultural treasure and represents Chinese art. It is reputed to be the most ancient artistic type in oriental world history. Calligraphy initially began due to the need to record ideas and information. The unique forms of calligraphy developed and originated from China, particularly for writing Chinese characters by using ink and a brush. Furthermore, Chinese calligraphy is responsible for the development of numerous forms of art such as ornate paperweights, ink stones, and seal carving.

The revivalist calligraphers of the Yuan dynasty such as Zhao Mengfu further developed the popular classical traditions of the Tang and Jin dynasties. In the Ming dynasty, the notions of artistic liberation and freedom from calligraphy rules gained momentum. During this period calligraphers started to form individual paths with their own styles.

During the Qing dynasty, scholars started turning to inspiration from the ancient works' rich resources inscribed in clerical and seal script. The Qing scholars were interested in studying these antiquities and becoming familiar with the steles that facilitated the creation of a calligraphy trend, which acted as a complement to the "Model Book" school. Therefore, the Stele school became a link between the present and the past in the approach to the traditions which the clerical and the seal script began being the Chinese calligraphy innovation sources.

The Four Treasures of Study

The four components of penmanship in ancient China, also known as "the Four Treasures of Study" were employed by scholars throughout ancient China.

Writing brush — It can be made from several different hair types, thus affecting how soft or hard it is which in turn impacts the style and breadth of each stroke. The nib can be made from rabbit's hair, wool, horsehair, or bristles, and so on; while the shaft may be made from bamboo, ivory, jade, crystal, gold, porcelain, ox horn, etc.

Ink stick — It comes in a long shaft, often decorated in delicate gold patterns and must be blended with water to create an ink paste. A good ink stick should be ground so as to be refined black with luster. With the invention of paper, they were improved accordingly.

Paper — It is one of the greatest contributions China made to the world. Before the existence of paper, our ancestors utilized knots in cords to record events. They then carved on bone, ivory, tortoise shell and bronzes. For very many years they wrote on pieces of bamboo and white silk. It was Cai Lun that invented paper. Today the Xuan paper originally made in Anhui Province still shines with its charm.

Ink slab — It is where the ink stone is ground with water and is often interestingly sculpted and quite heavy. Nearly all Chinese calligraphy enthusiasts hold that the star of ink slab is the *Duanyan*, ink slab produced in Duanzhou of Guangdong Province. It was always a tribute to the royal families during the Tang dynasty (618-907).

Categories of Chinese calligraphy

Over the centuries, different styles have evolved including seal script, clerical script, cursive script, running script, and standard script. Each script type has its own defining visual traits and lends itself to different kinds of textual content and function.

Seal script — The first script type to emerge in this sequence — was solidified during the Qin dynasty (221-207 BCE). The seal script signified authority, permanence, and orthodoxy, qualities befitting of the first imperial dynasty that unified China and standardized the writing system. Arranged in orderly columns, each character fits in an imaginary square. The strokes are of relatively even thickness, and the speed of execution is steady and slow. The solemnity of the seal script made it (and still makes it) a popular choice for commemorative titles carved onto the head of stone steles for public display or in frontispieces that announce the title of a handscroll painting.

Clerical script — It reached its height in the Eastern Han dynasty (25-220 CE). The character in general has a squatter silhouette when compared to its predecessor the seal script, introducing the possibility for greater rhythm in the composition. The strokes start displaying modulations and inflections (note the elegant flaring brush movement in the horizontal strokes), reflective of the different amount of pressure in the brush. This marks the calligrapher's conscious exploration of the brush's expressive potential. Clerical script takes less time to write than seal script, and it likely emerged out of a need for more efficient record keeping demanded by an expanding empire. The name for the script also suggests that it was initially used by government clerks. The clerical script is popular for commemorative texts carved into stone steles.

Cursive script — It is the most expressive of all five script types; it affords a calligrapher remarkable freedom thanks to this script's relaxation of the orthographic constraints of the seal and clerical scripts. Essentially an informal shorthand of the more complex forms of characters, cursive script was widely seen in epistolary writing, due to the expedient nature of its execution. Because the characters are more simplified, more freedom is allowed on the calligrapher's part to improvise and to take more liberty with the shape of the character. Since its maturation in the 4th century, the cursive script has been the choice for many master calligraphers to demonstrate their individuality. Calligraphy done in cursive script readily reveals the speed in which each character was brushed, sometimes so fast that two or more characters are interconnected by ligatures.

Running script — It combines the legibility of standard script and the expressivity of cursive script. The Song dynasty (960-1279 CE) with its literati calligraphers (scholar officials who obtained government posts after passing the civil service examination) saw a flowering of calligraphy in running script. This script became the preferred one for the greatest Song calligraphers because it lends itself to the trend at the time towards more personal even idiosyncratic styles. Calligraphy in this script type allows a wide range of speed in the execution of the strokes, and gives the calligrapher an opportunity to demonstrate familiarity with great calligraphers of the past. The Chinese calligrapher derives artistic legitimacy by demonstrating mastery of a repertoire of calligraphic styles that constitute the canon of Chinese calligraphy.

Standard script — The script type that most learners of Mandarin today encounter first during their studies — appeared the latest in the evolutionary sequence of Chinese calligraphy. Standard script reached its zenith during the Tang dynasty (618-907 CE) and it is associated with the moral uprightness of the calligrapher, due to its emphasis on the balance around a central axis in its form. It is the ubiquitous script for almost all kinds of printed media in the Chinese language, because it is the most legible of all five script types. Each character can be assembled using a standardized repertoire of brushstrokes that consist mainly of orthogonal strokes, making it fairly easy to reproduce texts in this script type using woodblock printing technology. It is fair to say that the standard script made a unique contribution to the dissemination of knowledge in premodern East Asia.

Closing words

Chinese calligraphy is an oriental tradition rooted in centuries of practice. It is an art of turning square Chinese characters into expressive images by varying the speed and pressure of a pointed Chinese brush. By controlling the concentration of ink, the thickness and absorptivity of the paper, and the flexibility of the brush, the artist is free to produce an infinite variety of styles and forms. In contrast to western calligraphy, diffusing ink blots and dry brush strokes are viewed as a natural expression rather than a fault. While western calligraphy often pursues font-like uniformity, Chinese calligraphy emphasizes more on expressing one's emotions. To the artist, calligraphy is a mental exercise that coordinates the mind and the body to choose the best styling in presenting the content of the passage. It is a most relaxing yet highly disciplined exercise indeed for one's physical well-being and spiritual cultivation.

(Adapted from *smarthistory.org*)

A6. Assignment

Theme Speech

You are invited to deliver a 5-minute theme speech on **Peking Opera** to a group of foreign tourists in China. Your speech might cover:

- origin and history
- face-painting and its symbolization
- roles and costumes
- renowned performers and plays
- significance of Peking Opera in the Chinese culture.

You may refer to the words and expressions in Part A, but don't confine yourself to them.

Part B Chinese Porcelain & Terracotta Army

B1. Introduction

The Highlights of Chinese Ceramics

China has an incredibly long and rich history of producing ceramics. Early examples date back more than 20,000 years predating Europe by at least 5,000 years. Indeed the very name "china" in English is a term for ceramics, particularly porcelain because for centuries this country was the only source for the world's finest ceramics. Another ceramic highlight is Terracotta Army which is also known as Terracotta Warriors and Horses. Both of them have displayed exquisite and masterful craftsmanship of the Chinese working people, and have shed light on the country's ancient artistic practices.

Chinese porcelain

The earliest porcelain-making started around the first century in China. The Tang and Song dynasties witnessed a time of rapid development in porcelain manufacture. Tri-colored glazed pottery of the Tang dynasty (618-907) is the finest among ancient Chinese pottery, and was often taken as the buried wares for emperors and nobles. Famous kilns emerged in multitude in the Song dynasty (960-1279), including the "Five Great Kilns": Ding Kiln, Ru Kiln, Ge Kiln, Guan Kiln and Jun Kiln, each with special and exclusive manufacturing skills and firing methods. The Ming dynasty saw the maturity of the art, and a large number of valuable pieces were produced in this period.

Jingdezhen, the Capital of Porcelain, produces up to over three thousand kinds of potteries, including artistic porcelain, porcelain articles for daily use and porcelain decorations, among which bone china is the best known. Blue and white porcelain, rice-pattern decorated porcelain, famille-rose porcelain (powder doped color decorated porcelain) and color-glazed porcelain are the "Four Great Porcelains" produced in Jingdezhen. Besides them, some others are also characteristic, such as statuary porcelain, eggshell porcelain and five-color porcelain. They are all choicest goods renowned both at home and abroad.

Chinese porcelain is cherished for its serene color, crystal paste, graceful designs and ingenious forms — a quest of generations of craftspeople. It is a comprehensive art, and form is as important to a good piece of porcelain as it is to a fine piece of sculpture. For porcelain ware of artistic value, an intriguing shape can capture instant attention from viewers. Chinese porcelain also pursues painting effects. Porcelain ware usually contains images from landscape or bird-and-flower paintings. Most porcelain craftspeople are also adept at painting. Elegance in shape, enchanting use of color, fine texture, and vivid images all set off each other, adding great splendor to the art.

Terracotta Army

Another iconic and impressive example of Chinese ceramics is Terracotta Army. Renowned as one of the greatest archaeological events in the twentieth century, buried at 1.5 km east of Qinshihuang's Mausoleum, Terracotta Army is the funerary object of Emperor Qinshihuang (259-210 BC), the first Emperor of China. The emperor built the Terracotta Army with the purpose of protecting and serving him in his afterlife.

They were discovered accidentally in 1974 when farmers drilling for water near the ancient city of Xi'an found the first shards of pottery that indicated their presence. Current estimates point towards that there all in all might be over 8,000 life-size pottery warrior figures, each including infantry and cavalry with spears, bows, 130 chariots and more than 600 horses. This extravagant but awesomely lifelike set of clay figures, most of which still remain to be excavated, reputedly took 700,000 workers over 38 years to produce. The three so far excavated pits are listed as a UNESCO World

Heritage site and are regarded as the Eighth Wonder of the World.

One of the most extraordinary features of the terracotta warriors is that each appears to have distinct features — an incredible feat of craftsmanship and production. Designed with an impressive level of detail, each figure is a one-of-a-kind work of art. The life-size sculptures vary in height according to military ranking, with their uniforms, hairstyles, gestures, and even facial shapes and expressions following suit. It represents unquestionably the finest collection of terracotta sculpture in the history of art. Sadly, over the intervening years between their burial and their discovery, the sculptures have lost nearly all of their decorative paint.

Closing words

Chinese ceramic ware is an art form that has been evolving since the neolithic period. Over the centuries, China maintained its dominant position as the world's preeminent producer of ceramics as countless new technologies and styles were developed. The above-mentioned examples are just two highlights of Chinese ceramics, serving as a superb paradigm of ancient Chinese art and a great legacy of the Chinese culture. They have promoted economic and cultural exchange between China and the outside world, and profoundly influenced the traditional culture and lifestyle of people from other countries.

(Adapted from *en.unesco.org*, *kevinpage.co.uk*, *worldhistory.org*)

B2. Words and Expressions

Vocabulary

1. china /ˈtʃaɪnə/ *n*. 瓷,瓷料;瓷器;瓷制品
2. ceramics /səˈræmɪks/ *n*. 陶瓷制品;制陶艺术;陶器制造
3. artisan /ˈɑːrtəzən/ *n*. & *adj*. 工匠,手艺人;以传统方式手工制作的
4. glaze /gleɪz/ *v*. & *n*. 给……上釉,使光亮;釉,釉料
5. kiln /kɪln/ *n*. (用以烧制砖块、陶器的)窑
6. cloisonne /ˌklɔɪzəˈneɪ/ *n*. & *adj*. 景泰蓝瓷器;景泰蓝制的
7. counterfeit /ˈkaʊntəfɪt/ *adj*. 伪造的,仿造的,假冒的
8. pinnacle /ˈpɪnəkəl/ *n*. 极点,顶点,顶峰;(建筑物的)尖顶,山顶
9. magnum opus /ˌmægnəmˈəʊpəs/ *n*. (作家或艺术家的)代表作,力作
10. necessitate /nəˈsesəteɪt/ *v*. 使成为必需

中国瓷器	Chinese Porcelain
精美的瓷器	fine china
保养很好的陶瓷制品	well-maintained ceramics
制作一件上好瓷器	make a piece of good chinaware
制瓷工匠	porcelain artisan
烧制温度	firing temperature
配比、成型、烘干和烧制	proportioning，molding，drying and firing
增加防水层	add a waterproof layer
精湛的技艺	exquisite artistry
擅长绘画	be adept at painting
雕刻花纹	engrave flower patterns
时尚的艺术品	stylish artistic ware
奢华的宫廷风格	a courtly lavish style
专属于皇室	exclusively for the royal family
达到它的鼎盛时期	reach its heyday
在历代王朝蓬勃发展	flourish throughout the successive dynasties
标记皇帝的统治年号	mark the reign name of the emperor
被制作于康熙年间	be made during the reign of Emperor Kangxi
著名瓷器生产地区	distinguished porcelain production area
瓷都	the Capital of Porcelain
“四大名瓷”：青花瓷、玲珑瓷、粉彩瓷、彩釉瓷	“Four Great Porcelains”：blue and white porcelain，rice-pattern porcelain，famille-rose porcelain and color-glazed porcelain
历史悠久的“五大名窑”：定窑、汝窑、哥窑、官窑、钧窑	longstanding “Five Great Kilns”：Ding Kiln，Ru Kiln，Ge Kiln，Guan Kiln and Jun Kiln
唐三彩	tri-colored glazed pottery of the Tang dynasty
景泰蓝	cloisonne
薄胎瓷	eggshell porcelain
五色瓷	five-color porcelain
单色釉瓷	monochrome-glazed porcelain
优雅的设计	graceful design
极具魅力的造型	intriguing shape
如玻璃一般通透	as transparent as glass
光滑无瑕的表面	smooth and unblemished surface
评估它的真伪和年代	evaluate its authenticity and age
查勘裂纹	inspect the crackles
形成铁锈斑点	form the rust spots

褪色	discoloration
中国古瓷收藏者	antique Chinese porcelain collector
仿制品	replica
仿造的古董	counterfeit antique
被高标准复原	be restored to a very high standard
艺术品的真品	genuine work of art
达到美的巅峰	reach the pinnacle of beauty
在西方受到高度评价	be highly prized in the West
大量出口欧洲	be heavily exported to Europe
订购定制的瓷器	order custom-made porcelain wares
来自古代中国的艺术奇迹	artistic marvel from ancient China
外交礼物	a diplomatic gift
作为文化载体	serve as a culture bearer
在雅俗之间广受欢迎	be widely welcomed among both refined and popular tastes
国内外知名的精品	choicest goods renowned both at home and abroad
成为中国文化的代表作	become the magnum opus of Chinese culture
用于艺术和装饰目的	preferable for artistic and decorative purposes
丝绸之路和茶马古道的贸易路线	trade routes on the Silk Road and the Tea Horse Road

Vocabulary

1. mausoleum /ˌmɑːzəˈliːəm/ *n*. 陵墓
2. megalomaniac /ˌmegələˈmeɪniæk/ *n*. 妄自尊大的人
3. sacrifice /ˈsækrəfaɪs/ *n*. & *v*. 祭品;以(人或动物)为祭品;牺牲,献出
4. life-size /ˈlaɪfsaɪz/ *adj*. 真人大小的;实物大小的
5. cavalry /ˈkævəlri/ *n*. (尤指旧时的)骑兵;机械化部队,装甲部队
6. inscribe /ɪnˈskraɪb/ *v*. 雕,刻;题写
7. accentuate /əkˈsentʃueɪt/ *v*. 着重,强调;使突出,使明显
8. lifelike/ˈlaɪflaɪk/ *adj*. 逼真的,惟妙惟肖的
9. exude /ɪgˈzuːd/ *v*. 散发,流出;充分显露(爱、自信、痛苦等)
10. artifact /ˈɑːrtəfækt/ *n*. (尤指具有史学价值的)人工制品,手工艺品

兵马俑	**Terracotta Army**
秦始皇帝陵博物院	Emperor Qinshihuang's Mausoleum Site Museum
最受欢迎的展览之一	one of the most travelled exhibitions
一个巨大的拱形大厅	a large arched hall
一座大型的帝王陵墓	a large-scale imperial tomb
蕴藏巨大财富	contain vast riches
在来世保护并服务于他	protect and serve him in his afterlife
建立一个统一的封建国家	establish a unified feudal country
为他赢得妄自尊大的专制者的名声	earn him a reputation as a megalomaniac despot
位居已知最早的遗迹之列	among the earliest known relics
保存最好的	best-preserved
用陶人来代替真正的人祭	substitute actual human sacrifices with pottery figures
试图重建一支真正的军队	attempt to recreate exactly a real army
随葬品	funerary objects
一号坑	Pit One / Vault One
一个完整的战斗队形	an entire battle formation
实物大小的战士和马匹	life-size warriors and horses
将零部件浇铸成型、烧制，然后组装并涂色	be molded in parts, fired, then assembled and painted
经过两千年的侵蚀和潮湿	after 2,000 years of erosion and humidity
失去原本鲜活的色彩	lose the original vivid color
全副武装的战士	armored warriors
步兵和骑兵	infantryman and cavalry
青铜战车	bronze chariot
驾驭战车者	charioteer
手握缰绳的骑士	horsemen holding the reins
直立的弓箭手	archers standing upright
身披战袍外穿盔甲	wear suits of armor over war robes
握着长柄青铜武器	hold long-staffed bronze weapons
剑、矛和弩	swords, spears and crossbows
上面刻有制造者的名字	be inscribed with its manufacturer
处于拉弓的姿势	in the pose of pulling a bow
个性化地塑造面部和发型	model the faces and hairdos individually
与他们的军衔一致	in accordance with their military ranks
不同的发型、姿势和面部表情	vary in hairstyles, gestures and facial expressions
在头右侧把头发盘成发髻	wear one's hair in a bun on the right side of the head

把头发编成辫子并在头顶盘成发髻	wear one's hair in a braid and form a bun at the top of the head
穿方头鞋	wear square-toed shoes
突出自己惟妙惟肖的特点	accentuate one's lifelike features
低垂的眉毛	lowered eyebrows
微张的鼻孔	slightly flaring nostrils
轻闭的嘴巴	gently closed mouth
睁大的眼睛	wide-open eyes
看起来强壮而警觉	look sturdy and alert
准备好一有战斗信号就出击	ready to strike at the first signal of battle
生活原型的真实再现	realistic representations of real-life models
没有任何夸张或扭曲	without any exaggeration or distortion
散发出一种动感	exude a sense of dynamic motion
代表高度的专业化	exemplify a high degree of specialization
参加海外展览	appear in overseas exhibitions
近距离观赏它的难得机会	a rare chance to view it up close
激发当代艺术家的灵感	inspire contemporary artists
一个伟大的考古发现	archaeological find
揭开古代军阵的神秘面纱	uncover the mystery of the ancient army array
持续进行的挖掘和修复	ongoing excavation and restoration
为墓坑提供良好的通风和日光条件以便保存	provide the pit with good ventilation and daylight conditions for its preservation
古代艺术品留下的不朽遗产	lasting legacy of the ancient artifacts

B3. Speaking Activities

Gift Design

You are going to give your foreign friend a piece of porcelain as a gift. Please design the porcelain gift in terms of its shape, color, floral prints, inscription, etc. Explain your design, originality and the message you aim to convey.

Debate

We may never know for sure what lies beneath Qinshihuang's mausoleum. Excavation revealed many mysterious findings, like strangely high levels of mercury and evidence that the poisonous substance coursed through an intricate system of underground troughs. It's been warned that the tombs were booby trapped, and modern archaeologists are kept away by the risk of damaging the site. Some artifacts could disintegrate rapidly if the tombs were opened.

(Adapted from *khanacademy.org*)

Topic for Debate:

Should archaeologists continue to excavate Qinshihuang's mausoleum?

Information Retelling

Study the picture below and try to retell all the information it displays in your own words. You will be given 5 minutes to prepare and you may add more details as necessary.

Why

An afterlife army for First Emperor Qin

The terra-cotta army was created to safeguard and serve First Emperor Qin in his afterlife. He wanted to have the same military power and imperial status in the afterlife as he had enjoyed during his earthly lifetime.

A show of First Emperor Qin's glory

It was built to remember the army he led to triumph over the other Warring States and unite China.

Substitutes for actual human sacrifices

Early rulers from the Shang and Zhou Dynasties had soldiers, officials and other attendants buried along with the dead emperor. The terracotta figures were produced to replace actual human sacrifices.

How

These warriors and horses all were built without advanced tools but by hand.

More than 700,000 artisans and laborers constructed the terracotta Army and Tomb Complex.

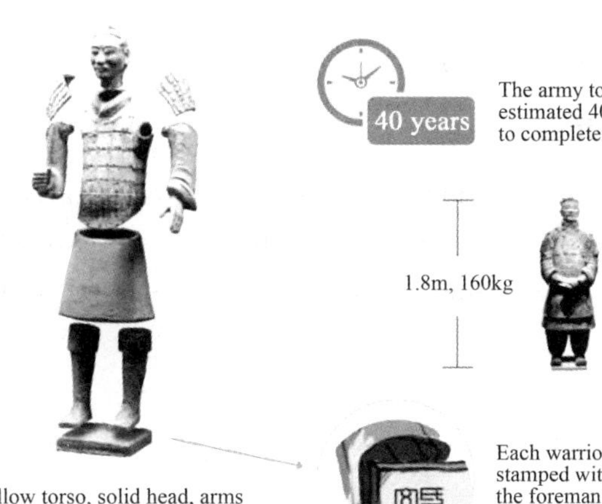

The army took an estimated 40 years to complete.

Hollow torso, solid head, arms and legs were created separately and then assembled.

Each warrior was stamped with the name of the foreman responsible for its creation, in order to track any mistakes.

(Adapted from *chinahighlights.com*)

Read and Share

Read the following paragraphs about **the restoration of Terracotta Army** and share your views.

Paragraph 1

When the clay warriors and horses of the Terracotta Army were unearthed, most of them were damaged either by natural factors or by human activities. For nearly 50 years, experts have been working to restore the life-size clay figures. The process of repairing a single piece usually takes months, or even years to complete.

Paragraph 2

The Qin Dynasty's craftsmanship was perfect with high aesthetic value. Restoration experts follow a principle of minimum intervention. They use an ultra-depth-of-field microscope to examine each piece and have developed a "paint layer reattachment" technique to restore the original color.

Paragraph 3

Over his 25-year career, Lan Desheng has helped restore more than 150 clay soldiers and horses. As more relics are discovered, the task becomes more challenging for a team of around 40 people. "There's an urgent need to involve more restorers, especially young ones with certain skills. I'd like to share with them what I've learned — that you have to make persistent efforts and endure loneliness. It's also important to be diligent, and do things in a down-to-earth manner, so that you can contribute to the protection of cultural relics," Lan said.

(Adapted from *cgtn.com*)

Ideas for Sharing:

- What role does modern technology play in archeological excavations?
- What does it take to be a qualified restorer of historical relics?
- Why is it worthwhile to spend so much time and energy on the restoration work?

Interpretation

Interpret the paragraphs below into English with the words and expressions you learned in Part B.

Paragraph 1

中国有悠久的制瓷历史,最早的瓷器制作始于公元1世纪左右。英文中"瓷器"(china)一词已成为"中国"这个国家的代名词。中国瓷器因其精湛的工艺、优雅的设计和巧妙的造型而受到珍视,这正是一代又一代工匠的追求。几个世纪以来,随着无数新技术和新风格的发展,中国一直保持着世界首屈一指的瓷器生产国的地位。

Paragraph 2

宋代是瓷器制造业最为繁荣的时期之一。当时的钧窑、哥窑、官窑、汝窑和定窑并称为五大名窑。拥有“瓷都”美誉的江西景德镇,在元代出产的青花瓷已成为瓷器的代表力作。青花瓷胎体质薄轻巧,如玻璃一般通透,光滑无瑕的白色瓷体上敷以蓝色花纹,堪称中国的艺术奇迹,在雅俗之间广受欢迎,并因此而大量出口海外。

Paragraph 3

兵马俑被誉为20世纪最伟大的考古事件之一,被列为世界文化遗产和世界第八大奇迹。它是中国第一位皇帝秦始皇的随葬品,这位皇帝建造兵马俑的目的是在来世继续保护和服务于他。据估计,这里共有8000多个真人大小的陶俑,他们身披战袍,外穿盔甲,手握青铜兵器,排成完整的战斗队形,宛如一支真正的军队。这些极其逼真的陶俑,大部分仍有待挖掘,考古工作仍在继续。

Paragraph 4

兵马俑中的人俑、陶马和实物一样大小,全部彩绘。所有的兵马俑雕塑,都非常真实,毫无夸张。每个人俑的面部神态、姿势、服装、发型及五官等各有特色。有的鼻孔微张,有的眉毛低垂,个个惟妙惟肖,富有动感。每个人物都是独一无二的艺术品,这体现了令人难以置信的高超工艺和生产水平。不幸的是,经过两千多年的掩埋和侵蚀,这些原本是彩色的雕塑在出土之后色彩多已脱落。

B4. Culture Highlights

Prized for its beauty, Chinese blue and white porcelain or Qinghua(青花瓷) is the nation's most famous china and also the most prevalent type of porcelain on the market. Throughout its history, artisans have continued to improve the way these wares are crafted and marked.

Q: *What is blue and white porcelain?*

A: It refers to a wide array of porcelain pottery painted with blue accents. Chinese potters crafted items from a native white clay called kaolin. Once hardened, the items were hand-painted with designs using blue cobalt pigment, coated with a clear glaze, and then fired in an extremely hot kiln. After firing, the finished pieces were quite delicate in appearance, but also very durable.

Q: *When did it originate and how was it developed?*

A: Chinese blue and white porcelain originated in the Tang and Song dynasties, but its technology didn't mature until the Yuan dynasty when they were first mass produced and rapidly developed. Potters of the subsequent Ming and Qing dynasties perfected these blue and white wares so that they soon came to represent the virtuosity of the Chinese potters.

Q: *Why was the Yuan dynasty so important to the development of blue and white porcelain?*

A: The Yuan dynasty was a special period for China and china. It was the first foreign-led dynasty in China. The fierce Mongolians not only captured an unprecedented territory, but also brought their ethnic culture, such as preference for the color white. Islamic culture also had a far-reaching influence on the Mongolian empire, and blue was one of the favorite colors of Muslims, as it symbolizes "the treasure in the desert" — water. Against this background, the Yuan dynasty's porcelain industry shifted its focus to blue and white porcelain.

Q: *Like other forms of pottery, blue and white porcelain was decorated with motifs that brought meaning to the piece. What were the most popular motifs?*

A: Many pieces contain motifs and decorations that offer wishes to the recipient, as porcelain was often given as a gift. Common wishes and example motifs include:

- Pine trees, peaches and cranes for longevity
- Fish for prosperity
- Deer for honor
- Mandarin ducks for happy marriage
- Pearl for granting wisdom
- Book for knowledge
- Coin for wealth
- Lotus flower for purification

Q: *How has China and even the world been influenced by blue and white porcelain?*

A: It has influenced Chinese aesthetics, with popular blue and white porcelain elements being applied to many products. For example, in the 2008 Beijing Olympic Games, a series of blue and white porcelain design uniforms were chosen for the medal ceremonies. Blue and white porcelain has been exported worldwide. It promotes economic and cultural exchange between China and the outside world, and profoundly influences the traditional culture and lifestyle of people from other countries.

(Adapted from *unesco.org*)

Terracotta Warriors and Horses is a magnificent collection of terracotta sculptures buried as the funerary objects of Qinshihuang, the First Emperor of China. Listed as the world cultural heritage site by UNESCO and the Eighth Wonder of the World, it is a must-visit attraction for all travelers to China. The clay-colored Terracotta Warriors is a mysterious wonder with many questions lingering behind. The followings are the top 5 facts you may not know about it.

1. Qinshihuang's burial complex was the largest in the world — and it was probably never completed.

Farmers digging a well in a field approximately 20 miles east of Xi'an stumbled upon a pit containing lots of life-size terracotta statues in March 1974. The site was soon identified as the burial place of Emperor Qin, and excavations began almost immediately. Historians now believe that some 700,000 workers worked for nearly four decades on the mausoleum. So far, archaeologists have uncovered a 20-square-mile compound, including some 8,000 terra cotta soldiers, along with numerous horses and chariots, a pyramid mound marking the emperor's tomb, remains of a palace, offices, store houses and stables. In addition to the large pit containing the 6,000 soldiers, a second pit was found with cavalry and infantry units and a third containing high-ranking officers and chariots. A fourth pit remained empty, suggesting that the burial pit was left unfinished at the time the emperor died.

2. All warriors and horses were made from clay and made by hand.

Most of the terracotta warriors remain vivid and complete, even though they suffered years of exposure. For decades, archaeologists have pondered how ancient artisans made such indestructible warriors in such a relatively short period of time, and they finally found out. The warriors were made from a kind of clay, which is very adhesive and easy to obtain. It can be found around the site. As technology was limited at the time, there were no advanced tools, and all warriors and horses were made by hand, step by step. Torso, head, legs, arms, and hands were all created separately. Then artisans would assemble them to create complete warriors. It usually takes at least two weeks to complete one terracotta warrior with this traditional method.

3. Each soldier in the Terracotta Army has distinct facial features.

The army of life-size terracotta soldiers, archers, horses and chariots was stationed in military formation near Emperor Qin's tomb in order to protect the emperor in the afterlife. The painstaking restoration of the figures — many of which were apparently vandalized soon after the emperor's death — revealed that they were creating using molds and an early assembly-line-type construction.

Though most of their hands are identical, and only eight molds were used to shape their heads, distinctive surface features were added with clay after assembly. As a result, each terra cotta soldier appears to be unique in its facial features, revealing a high level of craftsmanship and artistry.

4. Their weapons were extraordinarily well preserved.

During excavation of the pits containing the Terracotta Warriors, archaeologists have found some 40,000 bronze weapons, including battle axes, crossbows, arrowheads and spears. Even after more than 2,000 years, these weapons remained extremely well preserved thanks to protective chrome plating, a seemingly modern technique (first used in Germany in 1937 and the United States in 1950) that reveals the sophistication of ancient Chinese metallurgy.

5. The emperor's tomb itself still hasn't been excavated.

Even 40 years after its discovery, less than one percent of Emperor Qin's tomb has been excavated. Initial fears of damaging the corpse and the artifacts within the tomb later gave way to concerns about the potential safety hazards involved with excavation. According to an account by the first century BC. Chinese historian Sima Qian, entitled "The Grand Scribe's Records," mercury streams were inlaid in the floor of Qin's burial chamber to simulate local rivers running through his tomb. And in 2005, a team led by Chinese archaeologist Duan Chingbo tested 4,000 samples from the earthen burial mound for mercury; all came back highly positive. Given such historical and chemical evidence, debate continues over whether to excavate the tomb at all, and what methods should be used to best protect its contents as well as the people working at the site.

(Adapted from *history.com*)

B5. Extension

Synonym Discrimination

Can you figure out the differences among the words below?

Group 1: ceramics / porcelain / china / pottery

Group 2: artistry / craftsmanship / craft

Group 3: artisan / craftsman / artificer

Group 4: intriguing / enchanting / fascinating

Extensive Reading

Passage One

Chinese Porcelain

Why is porcelain called china?

As you stack the dishes into the dishwasher, or carefully arrange some flowers into your best vase, do you ever wonder exactly why many people refer to these articles as "china", and whether it has anything to do with the country of that name? The simple answer is "yes", the material is named after its country of origin.

Of course the name "china" does not necessarily refer to all pottery and ceramics, and not all ceramics originated in China. However, porcelain definitely has its roots in ancient Chinese expertise.

Many people are so inspired by the exquisite beauty of pieces of fine china, especially porcelain, that they are willing to not only pay a higher price for the utilitarian kitchen and bathroom commodities, but also to invest large sums of money in porcelain collectibles, both ancient and modern.

What is porcelain?

Porcelain is made from fine, white clay, known as *kaolin*, with added ingredients such as feldspar, and fired at a very hot 1260°C. The pieces are smooth and a translucent white, very strong and especially useful in the kitchen because of being non-porous, non-stick, and dishwasher safe. Porcelain is, not surprisingly, one of the most expensive kinds of pottery.

Quite apart from the durability of utilitarian porcelain pieces, the material has lent itself well to a host of artistic possibilities, and so the whole industry of porcelain collectibles has developed across the world with pieces both ancient and modern being traded for prices up to a record $84 million. Collectors look for the texture of the basic body, color of the glaze, decorative pattern, shape, and style of the pieces, as well as taking a special interest in the background stories of historical pieces.

Specific colors, patterns, and decorations are well known and sought after such as several blue and white possibilities, tri-color pieces, green celadon pieces, and the popular famille-rose porcelain from the Tang era. Every home contains some porcelain, in the bathroom at least. Many restaurants and kitchens rely on porcelain to prepare and present food. But the very best and most exciting porcelain can be found in museums and galleries, and collectors' display cases. Like all good art, it is loaded with both exquisite design and fascinating stories.

How is Chinese porcelain made?

A talented artist can create intricate and beautiful pieces with porcelain. However, if the materials are not selected and mixed just right, and if the firing of the work is not exactly correct, then the artist's efforts will be wasted.

The craft of making porcelain originated in China where the early makers used a type of clay called kaolin, and a type of granite called pegmatite. Nowadays it is made all over the world, and the main components are clay, specifically kaolinite, as well as feldspar and silica because in all of these the particles are extremely small. By varying the proportions of these ingredients, the properties of the porcelain can be changed.

Having been carefully selected, the raw materials need to be thoroughly crushed to make sure that all of the particles are extremely fine. The crushing is brought about using three types of equipment. Firstly, swinging metal jaws crush the material. Then hammer mills, which are rapidly moving hammers, grind it further. Finally, a ball mill, consisting of large rotating cylinders filled with steel or ceramic balls, further reduces the size of the particles.

The ingredients are then passed through a series of screens to make sure all of the particles are exactly the required size. Water is then added, forming a slurry, which is filtered with a magnet to remove any iron that may be in the mix. Iron is commonly present, and is undesirable because if it oxidizes it will turn the mix an unattractive reddish color.

Blue and white porcelain

To create this stunning style, firstly pieces are created as clean, shaped white clay, and bisque fired. The intricate blue designs are then painted on, usually with cobalt oxide. Then the piece is coated with a layer of transparent glaze before the final kiln firing.

Finally, the porcelain ware must be fired in a kiln. Some kilns have a single sealed chamber and can fire only one batch of ware at a time. However, the large commercial kilns are constructed inside a tunnel several hundred feet long. This way the ware can be moved from one zone to another, with each one continuously set to a particular temperature such as a preheating zone, a central firing zone, and a cooling zone.

The scientific basis for the firing process is complex, as firstly the carbon-based impurities are burnt out, particular chemicals decompose, and gases are produced which must be released from the ware. But eventually the feldspar and flint react with those decomposing minerals to form liquid glasses which shrink and bond the grains. Finally, as the ware cools, the liquid glasses solidify.

The porcelain product emerges from the kiln strong, white and translucent and ready to be used in so many ways. The artistic pieces emerge in all their delicacy and beauty, with the colors embedded in the strong, shiny glaze.

What is porcelain used for?

Maybe you have no desire to collect porcelain pieces, and you can't see the point in using "fancy" dishes at the dinner table, so you may think that porcelain use is not for you. But you might be surprised to realize how much porcelain actually affects your everyday life without giving it much thought. It seems like an old-fashioned material, and yet it has proved vital in so many ways in this technological era.

In ancient times porcelain was used firstly for household items, for preparing and serving of food. Porcelain utensils and dishes were observed to be impervious to liquid, durable even when heated, and also easy to clean and reuse. Soon porcelain items were being made for other minor household uses such as penholders and paperweights.

Decorative objects were created from porcelain, which could be used around the home as well as presented as gifts. Statues and ornate trinkets were created for wealthy people. Intricate porcelain articles featured as gifts in diplomatic exchanges. And as the rest of the world also discovered this remarkable material, porcelain was eagerly imported by the rest of the world.

Nowadays you can expect to see porcelain crockery as dinnerware, if not in your home then certainly in classy restaurants. There are also other places in your home where you definitely use porcelain. Firstly, there is the "water closet". Porcelain, sometimes referred to here as "vitreous china", is still the material of choice for the toilet stand because it is waterproof, clean, sanitary, as well as strong, rigid and very durable. It is easy to keep clean, and keeps an even temperature better than materials like stainless steel. And it is also the most popular material for your bathroom basin.

Porcelain tiles are popular for both floors and walls, especially in the bathroom, kitchen and laundry. Although porcelain is generally more expensive than other ceramic tiles, it has a lower water absorption rate, and is denser, and therefore harder, than other ceramics. In China, most floors and even external walls are tiled. Porcelain tiles can also be found on work surfaces, ledges, shelves, sills, and in some cases as roof tiles.

Another attribute of porcelain is that it does not conduct electricity, and as such it is used in the creation of insulators for electronic applications.

It is possible that you have some porcelain inside your mouth, as dentists often use porcelain for caps and crowns. These life-like tooth restorations made of entirely porcelain, are sometimes known as porcelain jackets. Even more durable are the porcelain-fused-to-metal crowns.

Despite its performance as a utilitarian product, it is the grace and elegance of the porcelain products that make them useful in a purely artistic way. People realized very early on, that porcelain pieces are so elegant in design and exquisitely beautiful, and yet durable, that they make great collectors' items. All over the world porcelain pieces, both ancient and modern, are collected and treasured as well as exchanged for large sums of money.

Naturally for those who are into collectibles in a big way, it is at least partly the unshakable investment value that makes porcelain most useful. But for many it is simply an attraction to the delicate artwork.

(Adapted from *chinaeducationaltours.com*)

Passage Two

Terracotta Warriors: An Army for the Afterlife

Owen Jarus

Chinese workers digging a well in 1974 made a startling discovery: thousands of life-size terracotta figures of an army prepared for battle. Now called the Terracotta Army or Terracotta Warriors, the figures are located in three pits near the city of Xi'an in China's Shaanxi province. After the warriors were discovered, the site became a museum and a UNESCO World Heritage Site in 1987.

The pits are situated less than one mile to the northeast of a pyramid-shaped mausoleum constructed for the first emperor of China, Qinshihuang (259 BC-210 BC). According to UNESCO World Heritage Center, archaeologists suspect that the unexcavated tomb could contain an entire replica of the city of Xi'an, which the warriors guard. The three pits (a fourth pit was unfinished) contain an estimated 8,000 life size terracotta figures of which about 2,000 have been excavated. The figures were created to serve the emperor in the afterlife and include a mix of chariots, cavalry, armored soldiers and archers. There are high-ranking officers (including nine generals found so far) and one of the pits, No. 3, actually served as a command post for the army and contains an honor guard and ornate chariot for the force's chief commander. All three pits are active archaeological sites and visitors can see excavations taking place.

The details of the warriors are so intricate and individualized that it has been hypothesized that they were based on real soldiers who served in the emperor's army. Each warrior has uniquely styled hair and features; some have topknots while others have goatees; some have caps and loose tunics while others have armored vests and braided hair. They have different builds, expressions and postures. Another key feature is that the warriors were decorated in bright colors, which contributed to the individuation. New conservation techniques, performed on recently excavated figures, allow some of these patterns to be discerned. Every warrior contains a stamp of the name of the foreman in charge of his creation, so that mistakes could be tracked.

Pit One: infantry and chariots

Pit One, the largest pit, is rectangular and covers 14,000 square meters of space, the size of almost three football fields. The portions excavated so far are filled with warriors. At the front of Pit One is a vanguard of un-armored standing archers, three rows deep, mainly equipped with bow and arrows. Behind them, separated by earthen mounds, are 11 straight lines of figures, many of them armored warriors who would have been equipped with melee weapons such as the halberd. Interspersed with these armored warriors are war chariots that were made of wood (now decayed) with four terracotta horses each. Each of these chariots has a driver (wearing extra-long armor for protection) along with two warriors armed with either melee weapons or bows.

This arrangement of a fast-moving vanguard, equipped with long-range weapons, which in turn is followed by a heavier force, is not an accident. Archaeologist Yuan Zhongyi points out in his book *China's Terracotta Army and the First Emperor's Mausoleum* that the ancient Chinese military strategist Sun Tzu wrote in his book the *Art of War* that the "the tip (vanguard) must be hard-hitting while the body must be overwhelming," a lesson the first emperor appears to have applied in the afterlife.

Pit Two: the cavalry

Pit Two is located just to the north of Pit One and is about half its size and roughly square. Emperor Qinshihuang was buried with everything he needed for the afterlife, including an army complete with life-size clay horses.

Like Pit One, its vanguard is made up largely of archers, in this case mainly carrying crossbows (again the wooden part is decayed). The figures in the front rows are un-armored and standing up, while the ones behind are kneeling. Again this is no accident, as Zhongyi points out that it takes time for an archer to load a new bolt for his crossbow. By having one line firing, and another kneeling to reload, a steady stream of fire could be kept up on the enemy.

The main force of Pit Two, the part meant to overwhelm the enemy, includes about 80 war chariots. Each has two riders and a charioteer and there are also some armored troops, equipped with melee weapons, intermixed.

Newly introduced in Pit Two is a squadron of cavalry. Located in the northwest of the pit, the saddled horses are male, life-size and each carries a rider. It's noted that the armor of the riders stops short of the waist, that way "the lap won't touch the horse when the rider is seated." The riders would have been equipped with both bows and melee weapons.

Pit Three: command post

By far the smallest of the pits is Pit Three, used as a command post. It has an honor guard consisting of armored warriors holding long poles. At center is a grand command chariot manned by four warriors. The beautifully painted vehicle body was crowned by a round ornamented canopy indicating that this chariot had a special function. It may have been designed to carry the commander of the army. The army commander is not included among the terracotta figures and researchers do not know his identity. One possibility is that the commander is no less than the emperor himself, who still lies buried in his tomb.

Non-military terracotta figures

Non-military terracotta figures have been discovered in other pits. Like the army, they were meant for the afterlife and include terracotta civil servants, equipped with knives and bamboo tablets for writing, and even a group of terracotta acrobats meant for entertainment.

"According to the way they [the acrobats] perform we speculate they are not indigenous to central China, but probably come from the south — probably the Burma area," said archaeologist Duan Qingbo, who was in charge of excavations at the Terracotta Army pits, in translated comments that appeared in "The Independent" (UK).

For the first emperor's afterlife, nothing was spared. He had a large army in proper military formation and even entertainment brought in from afar.

How were the warriors made?

For decades, archaeologists have pondered the techniques ancient artisans used to make thousands of individualized warriors in a relatively short period of time. Some have suspected that a single artisan produced each warrior; others hold that the individualized faces were achieved by attaching a unique mix of pre-determined ears, noses, mouths, etc. to the heads, a la Mr. Potato Head. One recent theory suggests that they were inspired by Greek sculpture techniques they learned from travelers on the Silk Road. Still others hypothesize that the warriors were created on an assembly line of convicts and conscripts. In this model, workers used molds for the body parts and heads, adding individual flourishes before sending the sculpture into the kiln. At least 10 different head molds have been identified.

In 2014, a group of researchers analyzed 30 ears from the warriors to determine how different they were from each other. They theorized that if the warriors were supposed to portray real people, they should have distinct ears (forensic scientists can use ear-shapes to identify people, similarly to fingerprints). No two ears analyzed were alike, though thousands more need to be assessed before archaeologists draw any specific conclusions. But it supports the theory that the warriors were based on a real army.

Mausoleum

The warriors are even more impressive when you consider that they are just one small part of Qinshihuang's mausoleum. Scientists have used remote sensing, core sampling and radar to discover that the tomb complex is almost 38 square miles. They suspect it contains a replica of the city of Xi'an, as well as its rivers and streams. In addition to clay inhabitants — warriors, acrobats, etc. — thousands of real people were also buried with their emperor. Many were craftsman and convicts who died building the mausoleum. Hundreds of concubines were also buried there, possibly to accompany their emperor to the afterlife, or possibly as part of an elaborate court intrigue.

Sima Qian's writings describe the contents of the tomb complex: "The tomb was filled with models of palaces, pavilions and offices as well as fine vessels, precious stones and rarities." Rivers and streams were made of mercury, hills and mountains of bronze, and precious stones represented the sun, moon, and stars. Tests on the dirt at the tomb reveal high levels of mercury, supporting Sima Qian's description.

But we may never know for sure what lies beneath the tomb. Sima Qian warned that it was booby trapped, and modern archaeologists are kept away by the risk of damaging the site. Some artifacts could disintegrate rapidly if the tombs were opened.

(Adapted from *livescience.com*)

B6. Assignment

Presentation

You are supposed to give a 5-minute presentation on **Chinese porcelain** to a group of foreign students at your university. Please make a PowerPoint to go with your presentation which might cover:

- development and evolution
- colors, images and shapes
- famous porcelains and production areas
- artistic value and practical use

- international reputation.

You may refer to the words and expressions in Part B, but don't confine yourself to them.

References

Beijing Opera. *TCT*. Retrieved from https://www.topchinatravel.com/china-guide/peking-opera.htm on March 4, 2022.

Chinese Calligraphy. *CHINA CULTURE TOUR*. Retrieved from https://www.chinaculturetour.com/culture/calligraphy.html on March 4, 2022.

Mark Cartwright. (2017). Ancient Chinese Art. *WORLD HISTORY ENCYCLOPEDIA*. Retrieved from https://www.worldhistory.org/Chinese_Art/.

Katriruishi. (2013). Peking Opera, a Gem of Chinese Culture. *Life in China Today*. Retrieved from https://lifeinchinatoday.com/2013/04/26/peking-opera-a-gem-of-chinese-culture/comment-page-1/.

Ai Yan. (2018). Peking Opera: Inheritance or Popularization? *CGTN*. Retrieved from https://news.cgtn.com/news/3d3d514f7845444d79457a6333566d54/index.html.

Learn Calligraphy — Step by Step Calligraphy Guide. *craft art*. Retrieved from https://craft-art.com/learn-calligraphy/ on March 4, 2022.

Ye Qing. (2021). Distinctive China: Mysterious and delicate Chinese facial makeup. *CGTN*. Retrieved from https://news.cgtn.com/news/2021-01-16/Distinctive-China-Mysterious-and-delicate-Chinese-facial-makeup-X6nxNhcW8o/index.html.

Jason Pae. (2014). Western Calligraphy vs. Chinese Calligraphy. *Prezi*. Retrieved from https://prezi.com/lh_l37x13sff/western-calligraphy-vs-chinese-calligraphy/.

Ann L. Silverberg. A Brief Introduction to Peking Opera. *Association for Asian Studies*, Retrieved from https://www.asianstudies.org/publications/eaa/archives/a-brief-introduction-to-peking-opera/ on March 4, 2022.

Dr. Xiaohan Du. (2020). Chinese Calligraphy, an Introduction. *smarthistory*. Retrieved from https://smarthistory.org/chinese-calligraphy-intro/.

Chinese Porcelain. *UNESCO*. Retrieved from https://en.unesco.org/silkroad/content/chinese-porcelain on March 4, 2022.

A Brief Introduction to Chinese Export Porcelain. *Kevin Page Oriental Art*. Retrieved from https://kevinpage.co.uk/news-and-blog/stories-behind-the-art/a-brief-introduction-to-chinese-export-porcelain/ on March 4, 2022.

Mark Cartwright. (2017). Terracotta Army. *WORLD HISTORY ENCYCLOPEDIA*. Retrieved from https://www.worldhistory.org/Terracotta_Army/.

Alexandra Nachescu. (2021). The Terracotta Warriors. *smarthistory*. Retrieved from https://smarthistory.org/the-terracotta-warriors/.

Lou Mo. (2020). Chinese Porcelain Compared & Explained. THE COLLECTOR. Retrieved from https://www.thecollector.com/chinese-porcelain/.

Restorers Bring Terracotta Army Back to Life. *CGTN*. Retrieved from https://news.cgtn.com/news/2021-05-07/Men-of-the-People-Restorers-bring-terracotta-army-back-to-life.

Sarah Pruitt. (2018). History Stories. *HISTORY*. Retrieved from https://www.history.com/news/5-things-you-may-not-know-about-the-terra-cotta-army.

Michael Sullivan. Chinese Bronzes. *Britannica*. Retrieved from https://www.britannica. com/art/Chinese-bronzes/The-Zhou-dynasty-1046-256-bce on March 4, 2022.

Fercility Jiang. (2021). The Top 12 Silk Facts for China Travelers. *China HIGHLIGHTS*. Retrieved from https://www. chinahighlights. com/travelguide/culture/silk-facts.html.

Owen Jarus. (2016). Terracotta Warriors: An Army for the Afterlife. *LIVESCIENCE*. Retrieved from https://www. livescience. com/25510-terracotta-warriors.html.

Candice Song. (2021). The Terracotta Army: A Complete Guide with Pictures & Infographics. *China HIGHLIGHTS*. Retrieved from https://www. chinahighlights. com/xian/terracotta-army/.

Ruth Wickham. (2020). Chinese Porcelain. *China Educational Tours*. Retrieved from https://www.chinaeducationaltours.com/guide/culture-chinese-porcelain.html.

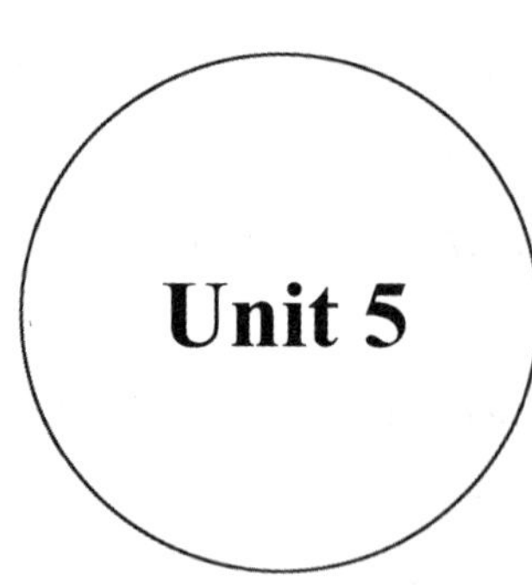

Traditional Thoughts and Beliefs

Part A Confucianism

A1. Introduction

Confucianism

Confucianism is often characterized as a system of social and ethical philosophy rather than a religion. In fact, Confucianism built on an ancient religious foundation to establish the social values, institutions, and transcendent ideals of traditional Chinese society. It was what a Chinese sociologist called a "diffused religion"; its institutions were not a separate church, but those of society, family, school, and state; its priests were not separate liturgical specialists, but parents, teachers, and officials. Confucianism was part of the Chinese social fabric and way of life; to Confucians, everyday life was the arena of religion.

The founder of Confucianism, Master Kong (Confucius, 551-479 BCE) did not intend to found a new religion, but to interpret and revive the unnamed religion of the Zhou dynasty, under which many people thought the ancient system of religious rule was bankrupt; why couldn't the gods prevent the social upheavals? The burning issue of the day was: If it is not the ancestral and nature spirits, what then is the basis of a stable, unified, and enduring social order? The dominant view of the day, espoused by Realists and Legalists, was that strict law and statecraft were the bases of sound policy. Confucius, however, believed that the basis lay in Zhou religion, in its rituals (li). He interpreted these not as sacrifices asking for the blessings of the gods, but as ceremonies performed by human agents and embodying the civilized and cultured patterns of behavior developed through generations of human wisdom. They embodied, for him, the ethical core of Chinese society. Moreover, Confucius applied the term "ritual" to actions beyond the formal sacrifices and religious ceremonies to include social rituals: courtesies and accepted standards of behavior — what we today call social mores. He saw these time-honored and traditional rituals as the basis of human civilization, and he felt that only a civilized society could have a stable, unified, and enduring social order.

Thus, one side of Confucianism was the affirmation of accepted values and norms of behavior in primary social institutions and basic human relationships. All human relationships involved a set of defined roles and mutual obligations; each participant should understand and conform to his/her proper role. Starting from individual and family, people acting rightly could reform and perfect the society. The blueprint of this process was described in "The Great Learning", a section of the *Classic of Rituals*:

> *Only when things are investigated is knowledge extended; only when knowledge is extended are thoughts sincere; only when thoughts are sincere are minds rectified; only when minds are rectified are the characters of persons cultivated; only when character is cultivated are our families regulated; only when families are regulated are states well governed; only when states are well governed is there peace in the world.*

Confucius' ethical vision ran against the grain of the legalistic mind set of his day. Only under the Han Emperor Wu (r. 140-87 BCE) did Confucianism become accepted as state ideology and orthodoxy. From that time on the imperial state promoted Confucian values to maintain law, order, and the status quo. In late traditional China, emperors sought to establish village lectures on Confucian moral precepts and to give civic awards to filial sons and chaste wives. The imperial family and other notables sponsored the publication of morality books that encouraged the practice of Confucian values: respect for parents, loyalty to government, and keeping to one's place in society — farmers should remain farmers, and practice the ethics of farming. This side of Confucianism was conservative, and served to bolster established institutions and long-standing social divisions.

There was, however, another side to Confucianism. Confucius not only stressed social rituals (*li*), but also humaneness (*ren*). *Ren*, sometimes translated love or kindness, is not any one virtue, but the source of all virtues. The Chinese character literally represents the relationship between "two persons", or co-humanity — the potential to live together humanely rather than scrapping like birds or beasts. *Ren* keeps ritual forms from becoming hollow; a ritual performed with *ren* has not only form, but ethical content; it nurtures the inner character of the person, furthers his/her ethical maturation. Thus, if the "outerside" of Confucianism was conformity and acceptance of social roles, the "inner" side was cultivation of conscience and character. Cultivation involved broad education and reflection on one's actions. It was a lifetime commitment to character building carving and polishing the stone of one's character until it was a lustrous gem. Master Kong described his own lifetime:

> *At fifteen, I set my heart on learning. At thirty, I was firmly established. At forty, I had no more doubts. At fifty, I knew the will of heaven. At sixty, I was ready to listen to it. At seventy, I could follow my heart's desire without transgressing what was right.* (*The Analects*, 2:4)

The inner pole of Confucianism was reformist, idealistic, and spiritual. It generated a high ideal for family interaction: Members were to treat each other with love, respect, and consideration for the needs of all. It prescribed a lofty ideal for the state: the ruler was to be a father to his people and look after their basic needs. It required officials to criticize their rulers and refuse to serve the corrupt. This inner and idealist wing spawned a Confucian reformation known in the West as Neo-Confucianism. The movement produced reformers, philanthropists, dedicated teachers and officials, and social philosophers from the eleventh through the nineteenth centuries.

The idealist wing of Confucianism had a religious character. Its ideals were transcendent, not in the sense that they were other worldly (the Confucians were not interested in a far-off heavenly realm), but in the sense of the transcendent ideal—perfection. On the one hand, Confucian values are so closely linked with everyday life that they sometimes seem trivial. Everyday life is so familiar that we do not take its moral content seriously. We are each a friend to someone, or a parent, or certainly the child of a parent. On the other hand, Confucians reminds us that the familiar ideals of friendship, parenthood, and filiality are far from trivial; in real life we only rarely attain these ideals. We all too often just go through the motions, too preoccupied to give our full attention to the relationship. If we consistently and wholeheartedly realized our potential to be the very best friend, parent, son, or daughter humanly possible, we would establish a level of caring, of moral excellence, that would approach the utopian. This is Confucian transcendence: to take the motions of everyday life seriously as the arena of moral and spiritual fulfillment.

The outer and inner aspects of Confucianism — its conforming and reforming sides — were in tension throughout Chinese history. Moreover, the tensions between social and political realities and the high-minded moral ideals of the Confucians were an ongoing source of concern for the leaders of this tradition. The dangers of moral sterility and hypocrisy were always present. Confucianism, they knew well, served both as a conservative state orthodoxy and a stimulus for reform. Great Confucians, like religious leaders everywhere, sought periodically to revive and renew the moral, intellectual, and spiritual vigor of the tradition. Until the 1890s, serious-minded Chinese saw

Confucianism, despite its failures to realize its ideal society, as the source of hope for China and the core of what it meant to be Chinese.

(Adapted from *asiansociety.org*)

A2. Words and Expressions

Vocabulary

1. sage /seɪdʒ/ *n.* 智者,贤人
2. allegiance /əˈliːdʒəns / *n.* (对国家或信仰的)忠诚
3. ethos /ˈiːθɒs / *n.* 道德思想
4. rite /raɪt/ *n.* 宗教仪式
5. benevolence /bəˈnevələns / *n.* 仁爱;善行
6. resurrection / ˌrezəˈrekʃ(ə)n / *n.* 复兴;复苏

孔子	**Confucius**
圣人	sage
至圣先师	sage of sages
雄心勃勃的青年学者	ambitious young scholar
弟子	disciple
《论语》	*The Analects*
《礼记》	*The Book of Rites*
五常	Five Constant Virtues
六艺	Six Arts
战国时期	the Warring States Period
春秋时期	the Spring and Autumn Period
贵族血统	noble ancestry
没有地位,处境卑微	be without rank and in humble circumstance
对老百姓有深切的同情心	deep sympathy for the common people
中央集权政府	centralized government
封建领主	feudal lord
名义上的效忠	nominal allegiance
法律与秩序	law and order
学习他的思想	study his doctrine
担任政府职务	serve in government post

辞去职务	resign his post
周游列国	set off on travel
自我流放	self-imposed exile
经历困难	undergo hardship
促进公共福利	promote the common welfare
因材施教	teach students in accordance with their aptitude
学无止境	live and learn
提高人文修养	improve one's learning of humanities
培养高尚品德	enhance one's virtue
拓展胸襟	broaden one's minds
提升精神境界	enhance one's spiritual ethos
仁、义、礼、智、信	benevolence, righteousness, ritual propriety, wisdom and trustworthiness
承担坚守和恢复伟大传统文化的使命	carry on the mission of sustainment and resurrection of the great cultural tradition
较早时期的价值传递者	transmitter for the values of earlier period

Vocabulary

1. propriety / prəˈpraɪəti / *n*. (行为)端正,得体
2. espouse / esˈpaʊz / *n*. 支持,拥护
3. obedience / əˈbiːdiəns / *n*. 服从;遵守
4. fidelity / fɪˈdeləti / *n*. 忠诚;忠实
5. hierarchy / ˈhaɪəˌrɑː(r)ki / *n*. 等级制度
6. fraternity / frəˈtɜː(r)nəti / *n*. 同好;博爱

儒学	**Confucianism**
哲学和信仰体系	philosophy and belief system
道德行为体系	a system of ethical conduct
奠定中国文化的基础	lay the foundation for Chinese culture
主导中国社会政治生活	dominate Chinese sociopolitical life
关注内在美德、道德和对社会的尊重	be concerned with inner virtue, morality, and respect for the community
生活的伦理指导	ethical guide to life
以人为本的美德	human-centered virtue

促进和谐,提高道德修养	promote peace and harmony and good morals
对生命原始状态的体会	a deep appreciation toward the original state of one's life
被作为一种精神来崇拜	be worshiped as a spirit
塑造品格	create the virtuous character
孝悌	filial and fraternal duty
尽孝	exercise one's filial piety
对家庭的奉献	devotion to family
尊重父母和祖先	respect for one's parents and ancestors
获得供养父母的物质条件	obtain the material means to support parents
维护兄弟间的团结	uphold fraternity among brothers
尊敬师长	obedience and deference to elders
社会等级	the hierarchies within society
仁	*ren* / benevolence / humaneness
信奉仁爱	espouse benevolence
与生俱来的	innate
利他主义的目标	altruistic goal
儒家理想状态的外在表现	outward expression of Confucian ideals
人类的爱和互动	human love and interaction
避免冲突	avoid conflict
推己及人	extend to other people
政治层面	political dimension
不人道的统治者	inhumane ruler
失去了天命	lose the Mandate of Heaven
君子	*junzi* / morally superior human being
修身、齐家、教化社会	cultivate one's behavior toward family and society
从政	enter a ruler's civil service
敏锐而深刻	sharp and profound
礼	li / rites
行礼	observe ritual propriety
宗教礼节	religious rituals
社会礼节	social etiquette
传统规范	conventional norm
丧礼	burial rituals
祭礼	ancestral worship rituals
祭祖	carry out sacrifice to the ancestors
以礼待人	display courtesy
严于律己	discipline one's conduct
敬业	perform duties of one's job

内化的适当行为模式	internalized model of appropriate behavior
定义合适的人类行为	define proper human conduct
自然秩序的衍生品	a derivative of natural order
人类的普遍价值	universal human values
四时运行	the rotation of the four seasons
万物生长	the growth of all living things
天道	way of Heaven
天德	virtue of Heaven
天命	heavenly mission
畏天命	respect one's heavenly mission
对天的敬畏和信仰	a sense of awe and belief in Heaven
重视自然力量	cultivate and center natural forces
生态文明	ecological civilization
建立天、地、人之间的和谐	establish the harmony of three realms —Heaven, Earth and Humanity

Vocabulary

1. anthology / æn'θɒlədʒi / *n*. 选集
2. embody / ɪm'bɒdi / *v*. 具体表现;体现
2. rotten / 'rɒt(ə)n / *adj*. 不适;腐烂的
3. lofty / 'lɒfti / *adj*. 崇高的,高尚的
4. virtuous /'vɜːtʃuəs/ *adj*. 道德高尚的
5. amend / ə'mend / *v*. 修正

《论语》	***The Analects***
孔子及其弟子的名言选集	anthology of quotes from Confucius and his disciples
体现了儒家传统的基本价值	embody the basic values of the Confucian tradition
阐明了道德和政治概念	illuminate moral and political concepts
由孔子的弟子们编撰的	be complied by disciples of Confucius
塑造了中国的思想和习俗	shape the thought and customs of China
无休止的自我实现过程	ceaseless process of self-realization
温故而知新,可以为师矣。	If a man keeps cherishing his old knowledge, so as to continually to be acquiring new, he may be a teacher of others.

学而不思则罔，思而不学则殆。	To learn without thinking, said the master, risks to be blind, while to think without learning risks to be impractical.
朽木不可雕也。	Rotten wood cannot be carved.
礼之用，和为贵。	In practicing the rules of propriety, appropriateness is to be prized.
己所不欲，勿施于人。	Do not impose on others what you do not desire yourself.
人无远虑，必有近忧。	He who does not think of the future is certain to have immediate worries.
过而不改，是谓过矣。	A fault that is not amended is a real fault.
君子喻于义，小人喻于利。	The gentleman knows what is right; the mean person keeps his mind only on gains.
逝者如斯夫！不舍昼夜。	Time passes away night and day like running water.
唯仁者能好人，能恶人。	Only the humane can love others and hate others.
父母在，不远游，游必有方。	While one's parents are alive, one should not travel to distant places. If it is necessary to travel, there should be a definite direction.
见贤思齐焉，见不贤而内自省也。	When one sees a virtuous man, one should think of exerting oneself to be like him; when one sees someone who is not virtuous, one should examine oneself.
志士仁人，无求生以害仁，有杀身以成仁。	A man with lofty ideals or humane man never gives up humanity to save his life, but may sacrifice his life to achieve humanity.
吾日三省吾身：为人谋而不忠乎？与朋友交而不信乎？传不习乎？	I daily examine myself on three points: whether, in transacting business for others, I may have been not faithful; whether, in intercourse with friends, I may have been not sincere; whether I may have not mastered and practiced the instruction of my teacher.
其身正，不令而行；其身不正，虽令不从。	When a prince's personal conduct is correct, his government is effective without the issuing of orders. If his personal conduct is not correct, he may issue orders, but they will not be followed.
知者乐水，仁者乐山；知者动，仁者静；知者乐，仁者寿。	The wise enjoy water, the humane enjoy mountains. The wise are active, the humane are quiet. The wise are happy; the humane live long lives.

三人行,必有我师焉。择其善者而从之,其不善者而改之。

When I walk along with two others, they may serve me as my teachers. I will select their good qualities and follow them, their bad qualities and avoid them.

诲女知之乎！知之为知之,不知为不知,是知也。

Shall I teach you what is understanding? To know what it is that you do not know — that is understanding.

子曰:学而时习之,不亦说乎？有朋自远方来,不亦乐乎？人不知,而不愠,不亦君子乎？

Is it not a delight, said the Master, to acquire knowledge and put it into practice? Is it not a pleasure to meet friends coming from afar? Is he not an intelligent man, who is careless alike of being known or unknown.

A3. Speaking Activities

Situational Speech

An international group tour will take part in a summit meeting in Qufu, Shandong province of China. You are invited to deliver a five-minute speech on **Confucius and Confucianism** at the meeting. Your speech might cover:

- The introduction of Confucius
- *The Analects* and its influences
- The core concepts of Confucianism

You may refer to the words and expressions in Part A, but don't confine yourself to them.

Role Play

Confucius and Socrates are twins in the history of philosophy. They lived in similar times and had comparable views; each was the founder of a great philosophic tradition. But neither wrote a treatise on the matters about which he was most concerned. The result is the existence of twin problems: what did Confucius really mean by *ren* (benevolence)? What did Socrates mean by wisdom? Imagine Confucius met with Socrates, and they had a philosophical exchange on such two problems. The conversation might contain:

- What is *ren*?
- What is the essence of *ren*?
- What is wisdom?
- How can one become wise?

Brainstorming

Confucius required people to hold Heaven in awe and claimed that a person of virtue must "respect his heavenly mission", listen to and live out the purpose of Heaven by caring for and improving life. Under the influence of Confucius, the ancient Chinese developed a sense of awe and belief in Heaven. In the 21st century, the Confucian caveat of "standing in awe of the ordinances of Heaven" still holds true, as human society begins to pay greater attention to ecological civilization.

- What is Heaven or *tian* for Confucius?
- Could you name at least five Chinese idioms about Heaven (*tian*)?
- How is Confucius' concept of Heaven related to the modern ecological civilization?

Read and Share

Read the following paragraphs about **filial piety** and share your views.

Paragraph 1

Filial piety (孝, *xiao*) is arguably China's most important moral tenet. A concept of Chinese philosophy for more than 3,000 years, *xiao* today entails a strong loyalty and deference to one' s parents, to one's ancestors, by extension, to one's country and its leaders. The Chinese philosopher Confucius (551-479 BCE) is most responsible for making *xiao* a pivotal part of society. He described filial piety and argued for its importance in creating a peaceful family and society in his book, *Xiao Jing*, also known as the *Classic of Xiao* and written in the 4th century BCE. The *Xiao Jing* became a classic text during the Han Dynasty (206-220), and it remained a classic of Chinese education up until the 20th century.

(Adapted from *thoughtco.com*)

Paragraph 2

In general, filial piety requires children to offer love, respect, support, and deference to their parents and other elders in the family, such as grandparents or older siblings. Acts of filial piety include obeying one's parent's wishes, taking care of them when they are old, and working hard to provide them with material comforts, such as food, money, or pampering. The idea follows from the fact that parents give life to their children, and support them throughout their developing years, providing food, education, and material needs. After receiving all these benefits, children are thus forever in debt to their parents. In order to acknowledge this eternal debt, children must respect and serve their parents all their lives. The tenet of filial piety also applies to all elders — teachers, professional superiors, or anyone who is older in age — and even the state. The family is the building block of society, and as such the hierarchical system of respect also applies to one's rulers and one's country. *Xiao* means that the same devotion and selflessness in serving one's family should also be used when serving one's country.

Thus, filial piety is an important value when it comes to treating one's immediate family, elders and superiors in general, and the state at large.

(Adapted from *thoughtco.com*)

Ideas for Sharing:

- What is filial piety? Why is it important today?
- Is filial piety still relevant today? How do you relate filial piety in your own family?

Debate

A prominent theme in Confucianism is education. Confucius himself devoted his whole life to teaching his disciples and persuading the political leaders of his time to enact his educational ideals. Confucius had a deep love of learning, education, and an unparalleled reverence for tradition and Chinese culture. Instead of working to instill that culture from a high government position as he had hoped, he traveled from place to place, teaching. He had a small group of followers that traveled with him from location to location, learning from him as well as helping him teach, and several of these followers took up important government positions after Confucius' death in 479 BCE.

(Adapted from *study.com*)

China has issued regulations for off-campus tutoring services banning private firms from offering after-school training in core school subjects. The new regulations ban local officials from approving new private education companies that offer after-school training on core subjects to elementary and middle school students.

(Adapted from *cgtn.com*)

Topic for Debate:

We should ban private tutors from giving online classes on core subjects

Interpretation

Interpret the paragraphs below into English with the words and expressions you learned in Part A.

Paragraph 1

春秋战国是经济、政治和社会巨大转变时期。这期间,经过长期的社会动乱和战争,古代沿袭下来的文化传统遭到破坏。孔子意识到这一点,并承担起坚守和恢复伟大传统文化的使命。《论语》是孔子言行的记录,由其弟子及其再传弟子记录整理而成。我们可以从《论语》中了解孔子的政治哲学思想。

Paragraph 2

《论语》认为，孝是人类情感的根本，它来自人对自己生命原始状态的体会。人们通过改善最初的家庭关系，增强自己的孝心。人类的爱心起初来自亲情，进而推己及人，将这份爱延伸到其他人身上，这就接近于博爱了。孝是仁的根本，如果人们认真体会孝之本，道就慢慢成长起来。

Paragraph 3

孔子提出"克己复礼"是实现仁的途径。人们应该认识到自己的私欲可能对他人造成不良影响，而且是有悖于礼的要求的。"一日克己复礼，天下归仁焉。"这句话的意思是，仁的目标并不遥远，人们想做就能够做到。只要待人之道长期得到正确的教育，人们就可以达到仁的境界，"为仁由己，而由人乎哉？"孔子认为既然仁是所有人都能够达到的理想，每个人都应该成仁。

A4. Culture Highlights

Q: *Ren (benevolence) and li (ritual propriety) are the two core concepts of Confucius' doctrine about people. What do they mean?*

A: The virtue of benevolence entails interacting with others guided by a sense of what is good from their perspectives. Sometimes *The Analects* defines benevolence generally as "caring for others", but in certain contexts it is associated with more specific behaviors. Examples of contextual definitions of benevolence include treating people on the street as important guests and common people as if they were attendants at a sacrifice, being reticent in speaking and rejecting the use of clever speech, and being respectful where one dwells, reverent where one works, and loyal where one deals with others. It is the broadest of the virtues, yet a gentleman would rather die than compromise it. Benevolence entails a kind of unselfishness, or, as David Hall and Roger Ames suggest, it involves forming moral judgments from a combined perspective of self and others.

The mastery that "ritual propriety" signaled was part of a curriculum associated with the training of rulers and officials, and proper ritual performance at court could also serve as a kind of political legitimation. Confucius summarized the different prongs of the education in ritual and music involved in the training of his followers:

Raise yourself up with the *Classic of Odes*. Establish yourself with ritual. Complete yourself with music.

On one occasion, Boyu, the son of Confucius, explained that when he asked his father to teach him, his father told him to study the *Classic of Odes* in order to have a means to speak with others, and to study ritual to establish himself. That Confucius insists that his son master classical literature and underscores the values of these cultural products as a means of transmitting the way from one generation to the next. He tells his disciples that the study of the *Classic of Odes* prepares them for different aspects of life, providing them with a capacity to: at home serve one's father, away from it serve one's lord, as well as increase one's knowledge of the names of birds, animals, plants and trees.

This valuation of knowledge of both the cultural and natural worlds is one reason why the figure of Confucius has traditionally been identified with schooling, and why today his birthday is celebrated as "Teacher's Day" in some parts of Asia. In the ancient world, this kind of education also qualified Confucius and his disciples for employment on estates and at courts.

(Adapted from *plato.stanford.edu*)

Q: *What is Confucius' ideology on education?*

A: The central place of education in Confucianism is stated in the opening passage of Xueji:

If a ruler desires to transform the people [and] perfect [their] customs, [the ruler] can only do so through education! (Xueji I).

The context of the passage is about good political governance. Rather than merely relying on laws, able officials, or virtuous advisors — all good measures in themselves — the ruler should devote attention to educating the people. The goal is to radically change the people by refining their conventional ways of thinking and doing. The reference to transformation and perfection in the above verse signifies that the scope is extensive, going beyond skills training and cognitive advancement to paradigm shift and character development. The actualization of this aim of education naturally requires a normative standard to guide the ruler in knowing whether and when the people have been transformed and their customs perfected. This standard is revealed in Xueji II to be dao (Way), which is the object of learning: "People who do not learn will not realize dao." Dao is the Way of Heaven (tian) or "guiding discourse" (Hansen, 1989) that is passed down from antiquity.

To realize dao is to understand and experience the "vision of human excellence" that forms the basis for human transformation and cultural perfection. As the normative tradition inherited from one's cultural predecessors, dao contributes to the formation of Confucian ideals and symbolic resources such as texts, cultural artifacts, and ceremonies. Dao was modeled and propagated by sage-kings such as Yao, Shun, and Yu of the first three dynasties of China (*The Analects*, 8.18, 8.19, 8.20, 8.21). Among the first three dynasties, the Zhou dynasty (1100-221 BCE) is singled out by Confucius as embodying dao through its cultural elements, such as the exemplary conduct of its rulers, institutions, and rituals. (*The Analects*, 9.5)

(Adapted from *oxfordre.com*)

Q: *What is Confucius' ideology on Heaven?*

A: In the Shang (1600-1046 BC) and Zhou (1046-256 BC) dynasties, the prevalent concept of "Heaven" was that of a personified god, which influenced Confucius. Generally, however, Confucius regarded "Heaven" as nature. He said, "Heaven does not speak in words. It speaks through the rotation of the four seasons and the growth of all living things." Obviously, Heaven equaled nature, in the eyes of Confucius. Moreover, nature was not a lifeless mechanism separate from humans; instead, it was the great world of life and the process of creation of life. Human life was part and parcel of nature as a whole.

Confucius' equation of Heaven with the creation of life was an innovative idea in his time. The natural process of life creation was the "way of Heaven." This idea was later developed in *The Book of Changes* (*Yijing*), as it stated "Continuous creation of life is change."

As the natural process of creation of life, Heaven was the source of all living things and the source of all values. This was the "virtue of Heaven." Thus, *The Book of Changes* said, "The great virtue of Heaven and Earth is creating life."

In the natural process of creation of life, Heaven had its inner purpose in creating all things as well as protecting and improving life. Heaven had originated humanity, and humans were obliged to accomplish this purpose. In other words, humans are born with a sense of "heavenly mission," and this is the meaning of human life. Confucian "Heaven" also had a certain sacred element, which was related to it being the source of life. Thus, Confucius required people to hold Heaven in awe. He says that a person of virtue must "respect his heavenly mission," listen to and live out the purpose of Heaven by caring for and improving life.

Under the influence of Confucius, the ancient Chinese developed a sense of awe and belief in Heaven. To them, Heaven was the highest sacred being, with its profound mystery never to be fully understood by mortals. It was not a supernatural, personified deity, but was the world of ever-generating life. As the most intelligent of all beings, humans should take to heart the purpose of Heaven by cherishing life. If one remained "ignorant and disrespectful of one's heavenly mission" by killing or maiming life, one would be punished by Heaven. Confucius said, "He who offends against Heaven has none to whom he can pray." The Confucian respect for and belief in Heaven represented a form of religious spiritualism of the ancient Chinese.

(Adapted from *simulation.toys*)

A5. Extension

Extensive Reading

Passage One

Ren & Li — Confucian Virtues

Ren and li are central concepts in Confucian ethics and form the first two of what are commonly called the "Five Constant Virtues" of Confucianism. Confucian philosophy emphasizes the role of moral development in determining who is fit to govern and lead society. As such, it focuses not only on adherence to rules and principles, but also the proper cultivation of moral character in all who would be governors.

Ren

Ren is translated into English as "humanity" or "humaneness." It is the highest Confucian principle. People cultivated by it are humane individuals who exhibit benevolence and care toward others. They are motivated by a deep empathy for others — what might be called "human-heartedness."

According to Confucius, all people have the capacity to be people of ren or humaneness mainly because all people are intrinsically good. This is a fundamental assumption of the Confucian worldview — that all people are inherently good and, thus, capable of operating in a way that is empathetic, humane and full of care for others. When people are not educated or developed properly, this intrinsic quality breaks down — people become hateful, rash, uncaring, undisciplined — and chaos comes into life at every level.

Through cultivation of Ren — of the capacity for empathy, humaneness, deep humanity — a truly "superior" human being emerges. Confucianism gives the term junzi to such superior human beings — a truly perfected person. Junzi are not perfect in the sense that they never make mistakes, but in the sense that their moral character is true, their intentions are pure, and their actions are disciplined and aligned with that moral character.

Li

Li is a companion virtue to ren in many respects — the other side of the same coin, soto speak. It is translated as "ritual" "propriety" or "etiquette." It is this dimension of Confucian philosophy and ethics that makes it "religious" more than anything else — the element of ritual.

Confucius was a conservative — he believed in tradition and in conserving and respecting tradition. Therefore, respect for rituals, traditional practices and conventional mores became important in his thought for restoring and maintaining order in society. And these rituals extend throughout all of life — the imperial palace, the marketplace, and the home.

Li is the mechanism by which all of life is ritualized and declared "sacred" in a sense. Through it, life is properly ordered and harmony is established. Although the concept of li existed in ancient ritualized ancestor worship in a limited and narrowly religious form, Confucius broadened it to apply to all activities in life so that all of life takes on the air of religiousness or seriousness. Bowing in greeting to someone, wearing certain colors of clothing on certain days, behaving in certain ways around those older than you, observing proper manners at a meal or meeting, and so much more — all these are examples of li in everyday life.

Ren & Li Combined

"*To master and control the self and return to li, that is Ren.*"(*The Analects*, 12.1)

Together, these two virtues create a highly cultivated and disciplined person who behaves properly in every situation and who is motivated by deep care and empathy for people. This person is the *junzi*, or superior person, mentioned above. They control their actions, impulses and desires in accordance with the demands of li and ren. As such, they exhibit a strong sense of personal power — called de (virtue) in Confucianism — that compels people to follow their example.

This exceptional quality, combined with other knowledge and skill, makes them the ideal people to create and govern a harmonious society. For this reason, the entire corpus of Confucian teaching, texts and traditions in focused on the cultivation of moral character in people who have the intellectual capacity to learn the things necessary for government. Intellectual capacity alone for leaders and governors is not sufficient; moral character must accompany it, otherwise these governors and leaders will drive society into lawlessness and chaos.

(Adapted from *world-religions-professors.com*)

Passage Two

Development and Legacy of Confucius's Thoughts

Confucius was a 6th century BCE Chinese philosopher. His thoughts, expressed in the philosophy of Confucianism, have influenced Chinese culture right up to the present day. Confucius is a larger-than-life figure and it is difficult to separate reality from myth. Considered the first teacher, his teachings are expressed in short phrases which are open to various interpretations.

Chief among his philosophical ideas is the importance of a virtuous life, filial piety and ancestor worship. Also emphasized is the necessity for benevolent and frugal rulers, the importance of inner moral harmony and its direct connection with harmony in the physical world and that rulers and teachers are important role models for wider society.

Confucius' early Life

Confucius is believed to have lived from 551 to 479 BCE in the state of Lu (now Shandong Province or Shantung). However, the earliest written record of him dates from some four hundred years after his death in the Historical Records of Sima Qian. Raised in the city of Qufu (or K'u-fou), Confucius worked for the Prince of Lu in various capacities, notably as the Director of Public Works in 503 BCE and then the Director of the Justice Department in 501 BCE. Later, he travelled widely in China and met with several minor adventures including imprisonment for five days due to a case of mistaken identity. Confucius met the incident with typical restraint and was said to have calmly played his stringed instrument until the error was discovered.

Eventually, Confucius returned to his hometown where he established his own school in order to provide students with the teachings of the ancients. Confucius did not consider himself a "creator" but rather a "transmitter" of these ancient moral traditions. Confucius' school was also open to all classes, rich and poor.

Confucius' works

It was whilst he was teaching in his school that Confucius started to write. Two collections of poetry were the *Book of Odes* (Shijing or Shi King) and the *Book of Documents* (Shujing or Shu king). *The Spring and Autumn Annals* (Lin Jing or Lin

King), which told the history of Lu, and the *Book of Changes* (Yi Jing or Yi King) was a collection of treatises on divination. Unfortunately for posterity, none of these works outlined Confucius' philosophy. Confucianism, therefore, had to be created from second-hand accounts and the most reliable documentation of the ideas of Confucius is considered to be *The Analects*. The other three major sources of Confucian thought are Mencius, Great Learning and Mean. With *The Analects*, these works constitute the *Four Books of Confucianism* otherwise referred to as the *Confucian Classics*.

Mencius & Xunzi

The thoughts of Confucius were further developed and codified by two important philosophers, Mencius (or Mengzi) and Xunzi (or Hsun Tzu). Whilst both believed that man's sense of morality and justice separated him from the other animals, Mencius expounded the belief that human nature is essentially good whilst Xunzi, although not of an opposite position, was slightly more pessimistic about human nature and he, therefore, stressed the importance of education and ritual to keep people on the right moral track.

Confucianism, therefore, expounded the importance of four virtues which we all possess: benevolence, righteousness, observance of rites and moral wisdom. A fifth was later added faith — which neatly corresponded to the five elements (in Chinese thought) of earth, wood, fire, metal and water. Once again, the belief that there is a close link between the physical and moral spheres is illustrated. By stating that all men have such virtues, two ideas are consequent: education must nurture and cultivate them and all men are equal — "Within the four seas all men are brothers". With suitable application and proper behavior, anyone can become a sage (*sheng*). It is not innate talent which is important but one' s will to mold one' s character into the most virtuous possible.

Legacy

Following his death in 479 BCE, Confucius was buried in his family' s tomb in Qufu (in Shandong) and, over the following centuries, his stature grew so that he became the subject of worship in schools during the Han Dynasty (206 BCE-220 CE) and temples were established in his name at all administrative capitals during the Tang Dynasty (618-907 CE). Throughout the imperial period an extensive knowledge of the fundamental texts of Confucianism was a necessity in order to pass the civil service selection examinations. Educated people and aristocratic families often had a tablet of Confucius' writings prominently displayed in their houses and sometimes also statues, most often seated and dressed in imperial costume to symbolize his status as "the king without a throne". Portrait prints were also popular, especially those taken from the lost original attributed to Wu Daozi and made in the 8th century CE. Unfortunately, no contemporary portrait of Confucius survives but he is most often portrayed as a wise old man with long grey hair and moustaches, sometimes carrying scrolls.

The teachings of Confucius and his followers have, then, been an integral part of Chinese education for centuries and the influence of Confucianism is still visible today in contemporary Chinese culture and other East Asian cultures with its continued emphasis on family relationships, filial piety and respect, the importance of rituals, the value given to restraint and ceremonies, and the strong belief in the power and benefits of education.

(Adapted from *worldhistory.org*)

A6. Assignment

Poster Design

Form groups of 3 or 4 and **design an English poster on Confucius and Confucianism** based on the following outline.

Bibliographical Fact about Confucius:
Confucius's Philosophy & Vision:
Confucius's Accomplishments:
The Significance of Confucianism:

Part B Daoism and the *Tao-Te-Ching*

B1. Introduction

Daoism: The Way

During its entire history, Daoism has coexisted alongside the Confucian tradition, which served as the ethical and religious basis of the institutions and arrangements of the Chinese empire. Daoism, while not radically subversive, offered a range of alternatives to the Confucian way of life and point of view. These alternatives, however, were not mutually exclusive. For the vast majority of Chinese, there was no question of choosing between Confucianism and Daoism. Except for a few straight laced Confucians and a few pious Daoists, the Chinese man or woman practiced both — either at different phases of life or as different sides of personality and taste.

Classical Daoist philosophy, formulated by Laozi, the anonymous editor of the *Tao-Te-Ching*, and Zhuangzi, was interpretation and development of an ancient nameless tradition of nature worship and divination. Laozi and Zhuangzi, living at a time of social disorder and great religious skepticism, developed the notion of the Dao (Dao —way, or path) as the origin of all creation and the force — unknowable in its essence but observable in its manifestations — that lies behind the functioning and changes of the natural world. They saw in Dao and nature the basis of a spiritual approach to living.

This, they believed, was the answer to the burning issue of the day: what is the basis of a stable, unified, and enduring social order? The order and harmony of nature, they said, was far more stable and enduring than either the power of the state or the civilized institutions constructed by human learning. Healthy human life could flourish only in accord with Dao, a free-and-easy approach to life. The early Daoists taught the art of living and surviving by conforming with the natural way of things; they called their approach to action wuwei (literally, "no-action"), action modeled on nature. To be skillful and creative, they had to have inner spiritual concentration and put aside concern with externals, such as monetary rewards, fame, and praise. Art, like life, followed the creative path of nature, not the values of human society.

Throughout Chinese history, people weary of social activism and aware of the fragility of human achievements would retire from the world and turn to nature. They might retreat to a countryside or mountain setting to commune with natural beauty. They would compose or recite poetry about nature, or paint a picture of the scene, attempting to capture the creative forces at the center of nature's vitality. They might share their outing with friends, drinking a bit of wine, and enjoying the autumn leaves or the moon.

If Daoist ideas and images inspired in the Chinese a love of nature and an occasional retreat to it from the cares of the world to rest and heal, it also inspired an intense affirmation of life: physical life — health, well-being, vitality, longevity, and even immortality. Some Daoists searched for "isles of the immortals", or for herbs or chemical compounds that could ensure immortality. More often, Daoists were interested in health and vitality; they experimented with herbal medicine and pharmacology, greatly advancing these arts; they developed principles of macrobiotic cooking and other healthy diets; they developed systems of gymnastics and massage to keep the body strong and youthful. Daoists were supporters both of magic and of proto-science; they were the element of Chinese culture most interested in the study of and experiments with nature.

(Adapted from *asiansociety.org*)

B2. Words and Expressions

Vocabulary

1. cosmic / ˈkɒzmɪk / *adj*. 宇宙的
2. archive / ˈɑːkaɪv / *n*. 档案
3. legendary / ˈledʒdəri / *adj*. 传奇的；赫赫有名的
4. indigenous /ɪndɪdʒənəs / *adj*. 本土的
5. cyclical / sɪklɪk(ə)l / *adj*. 周期的；循环的

道家	**Daoism**
道家学派代表人物	a key figure of Daoism
自然哲学家	natural philosopher
老子	Laozi / Lao Tzu
庄子	Zhuangzi / Chuang Tzu
诸子百家	the Hundred Schools of Thought
中国思想的黄金时期	the Golden Age of Chinese thought
文化与智慧的扩展	cultural and intellectual expansion
守藏室之史	an official in the imperial archives
一个半传奇式的人物	a semi-legendary figure

带着浓厚的宗教色彩	take on strong religious overtone
见证周朝的衰落	witness the decline of *Zhou*
流亡	go into exile
掌管边关的官员	official in charge of the border crossing
把他的教义写成文字	put his teaching into writing
《道德经》	*Tao-Te-Ching*
本土宗教	indigenous religion
以"道"为核心的哲学体系	a philosophy system centered on Tao
理想准则	ideals and norms
宇宙之源	cosmic origin
宇宙论思想	cosmological thought
对自然界的观察	an observance of the natural world
秩序的内在原则	the inherent principle of order
自然界的物理世界	physical world of nature
宇宙的运转规律	the way of the universe
季节的交替	the alternation of the season
植物和动物的生长周期	growth cycle of plants and animals
阴阳转变	yin-yang interchanging
宇宙中不可分割的一部分	inseparable part of the universe
从阴阳学派中汲取其宇宙论概念	draw its cosmological notions from the School of Yinyang
提高精神意识	heightened spiritual awareness
根据自然界的交替循环来调整	in accordance with the alternating cycles of nature
根据宇宙的脉搏调整节奏	adjust the rhythm to the pulse of the cosmos
与变化的周期脱节	out of rhythm with the cycles of change
破坏了和谐	disrupt the harmony

Vocabulary

1. reverence / ˈrevərəns / *n*. 尊敬;崇敬
2. spontaneous / spɒnˈteɪniəs / *adj*. 自发的;非勉强的
3. metaphor / ˈmetəfɔːr / *n*. 隐喻;暗喻
4. ingenuity / ˌɪndʒəˈnjuːəti / *n*. 聪明才智;独创力
5. tenacity / təˈnæsəti / *n*. 坚韧;顽强
6. emancipation / ɪˌmænsɪˈpeɪʃ(ə)n / *n*. 解放

道家理论	Principles of Daoism
无为	wuwei / nonaction
无为而治	action in non-action
对自然界的敬畏	reverence for the natural world
让我们的行为成为自发的、必然的	make our behavior as spontaneous and inevitable
顺水推舟	swim with current
不执着于自我的想法中	non-clinging to the idea of an individual ego
以水为主要喻体	employ water as chief metaphor
无处不在	omnipresent
遵循自己的路线	follow its own course
忠于自己	be true to yourself
保持低调	maintain a low profile
不争	non-contention
无形	shapelessness
无名	namelessness
玄妙	obscurity
心斋	mindfasting
坚韧	tenacity
相反,反面	reversion; opposition
反者道之动	The motion of Dao is transforming into the opposite or returning to the original state
复归于"婴儿"	return to a "new baby" state
真实生命的呼唤	the call of genuine life
虚假,虚伪	hypocritical
"本色"的背离	a departure from the "true self"
崇尚自然	worshiping the nature
空无一物的状态	a state of emptiness
大智若愚。	Great ingenuity appears to be stupidity
以柔克刚	overcoming the strong by being weak
顺应自然	follow the way of nature
无欲则刚。	One is invincible because he desires nothing and contends for nothing.
返璞归真	return to the state of a newborn baby
滴水穿石。	Constant dropping wears the stone.
反向思考	think through opposition
玄之又玄	the obscurest of the obscure
弱小和服从的力量	the power of being weak and yielding

人的精神解放	spiritual emancipation of humanity
不战而屈人之兵。	Win a war without fighting it.
人往高处走，水往低处流。	Humans tend to seek higher positions while water always flows to lower places.
天地与我并生，而万物与我为一。	The universe and I came into being together; I and everything therein are One.
与自然融为一体	the sensibility of being integrated with nature
归向自然，恢复人的本性	the return of one's suppressed soul back to nature

Vocabulary

1. elusiveness / iˈluːsɪv / *adj*. 难以描述的
2. secular / ˈsekjʊlə(r) / *adj*. 现世的；世俗的
3. volition / vəˈlɪʃ(ə)n / *n*. 意志力
4. subtle /ˈsʌtl/ *adj*. 不易察觉的；不明显的
5. aesthetic / iːsˈθetɪk / *adj*. 审美的；美学的
6. fringe / frɪndʒ / *adj*. 外围

《道德经》	***Tao-Te-Ching***
道	the way
德	virtue
中国哲学文献的经典	classic of Chinese philosophical literature
提出一种生活方式	present a way of life
恢复和谐与安宁	restore harmony and tranquility
有不同的解释	receive a wide variety of interpretations
其难以捉摸和神秘的色彩	its elusiveness and mystical overtone
修身	self-cultivation
治国	state governing
对立统一	unity of opposites
治国之道	the art of governance
理想的社会秩序	ideal social order
世俗生活	secular life
自然法则	law of nature
主观意志	subjective volition
天地万物之源	the source of all things

民族特性	national characteristics
思想倾向	trends of thought
审美趣味	aesthetic sensibilities
道可道,非常道。	The Tao that can be described is not the enduring and unchanging Tao.
名可名,非常名。	The name that can be named is not the enduring and unchanging name.
无名天地之始,有名万物之母。	(Conceived of as) having no name, it is the Originator of heaven and earth; (Conceived of as) having a name, it is the Mother of all things.
故常无欲,以观其妙。	Always without desire we must be found. If its deep mystery we would sound;
常有欲,以观其徼。	But if desire always within us be. Its outer fringe is all that we shall see.
此两者同出而异名,同谓之玄。	Under these two aspects, it is really the same; but as development takes place, it receives the different names. Together we call them the Mystery.
玄而又玄,众妙之门。	Where the Mystery is the deepest is the gate of all that is subtle and wonderful.
道隐无名。	The Way conceals itself in being nameless.
人法地,地法天,天法道,道法自然。	Man patterns himself after earth; earth patterns itself after heaven. Heaven patterns itself after Dao; Dao patterns itself after naturalness.
夫唯不争,故天下莫能与之争。	As he contends for nothing, none in the world could contend with him.
圣人之道,为而不争。	The Dao of the sage is to do what he can but contend with none.
吾不知其名,字之曰道。	Its true name, I do not know; Way or Dao is the byname we give.

B3. Speaking Activities

Situational Speech

Your university is going to hold a book fair on ancient Chinese philosophy. You are invited to deliver a five-minute speech on the ***Tao-Te-Ching*** to foreign students. Your speech might cover:

- Basic principles of the *Tao-Te-Ching*
- The current status of the *Tao-Te-Ching*

- Cultural influences of the *Tao-Te-Ching*

You may refer to the words and expressions in Part A, but don't confine yourself to them.

Role Play

Laozi was a man of great learning. Even Confucius was said to have traveled miles to consult him. Imagine you were a student of Confucius and you need to consult him. Your questions might contain:

- What are the major principles of Laozi?
- How does he understand "Great ingenuity appears to be stupidity"?
- What are the major differences between his thoughts and Confucius's?

Brainstorming

The following are the different ways of translation of basic viewpoints of Lao Tzu. Which way do you prefer and why?

道	无为	不争	有/无
Dao, Tao Way, Way-making Road Divine law	Non-action Nothingness Wuwei	Non-contention No competition No-fighting	Being Non-being You / Wu

Read and Share

Read the following paragraphs about **wu wei** and **tang ping.** Share your views.

Paragraph 1

Wu wei is a Taoist concept that means "non-action". It's a philosophy which states that the best way to deal with a situation, especially with a conflict, is not to act at all. Moreover, not forcing any solution, but just letting things flow. Most of us find a philosophy that teaches us non-action strange. We live in a society that constantly induces us to do the opposite. In fact, we're living a life full of things to do, feelings, and thoughts. And when we're doing nothing, we feel strange. We would think that this is simply a waste of time.

Wu wei proposes a simple way of life because this translates into peace and harmony. This simplicity means not getting too attached to ambitions and desires since they're the major sources of chaos and suffering, rather than understanding.

Simplicity also helps us live in a more peaceful way. This is impossible when we're focused on achieving great things. It's about valuing what we are and what we have instead of complaining about what we aren't or don't have.

In the same way, the wu wei argues that simplicity helps us accept things as they are, not resist the course of events, nor pretend to take control over them. These are values and attitudes that contradict the Western mentality, but which cultivate greater emotional balance.

(Adapted from *exploringyourmind.com*)

Paragraph 2

Tang ping describes a longing to escape the pressures of modern life in China, where young people are expected to work long hours, buy property, get married and have children. Many people in their 20s and 30s grumble that hard work no longer rewards them with a better quality of life. They have adopted an academic term, nei juan or "involution", to describe how extra input no longer yields more output. Unlike their parents, who enjoyed a booming economy, they feel that society is stagnating and inequality growing.

Other ways of expressing this mood have also become common. One is sang, or "dejected": many young people now talk of the spread of a "sang culture" in China. They refer to "Buddhist youth", meaning those who are never disappointed since they want nothing. Some young Chinese call themselves chives, harvested or exploited by firms. As they point out online, it is difficult to harvest chives when they are lying flat.

(Adapted from *The Economist*)

Ideas for Sharing:

- What are the differences between wu wei and tang ping?
- Are there any connections between the two?
- What are your suggestions for those faced with great pressures?

Interpretation

Interpret the paragraphs below into English with the words and expressions you learned in Part A.

Paragraph 1

《道德经》的深刻之处在于,它提示人们不但要去面对他们与世界的关系,而且还要把这种关系揭示出来,得出结论。老子提倡与自然融为一体,而不需要语言系统或者表达方式。借此,老子引入一种特殊的讲道方式,即所有能够写下来的并不是道本身。道是变化的、运动的,但又是相对恒常的。名称也一样,如果你给予某件东西以名字的话,那它就不是那个字面上的名字所指的东西。然而,人类又不得不通过语言和表达系统与世界打交道。

Paragraph 2

老子告诉人们反向的道理,这说明在一些方面他比孔子显得更加深刻。孔子教导人们应该做什么和如何去做,而老子则教授人们事物皆具有反面性的道理。通过对水的领悟,老子重视弱小和服从的力量。没有多少人能够理解弱能够胜强的道理,也没有多少人能够做人行事遵循这个规律。这不意味着如果人们理解了事物的一面,另一面就不言而喻地自己说明一切。实际上,事物没有一面能够离得开另外一面而独立存在的。道总是向相反方向运动,并存在于逐渐变弱的过程中。水是柔弱的,但是它也可以极具破坏性。洪水是危险的,而滴水也可以穿石。水之所以威力强大,是因为水具有无法比拟的坚韧性。

Paragraph 3

道的本意是指人们走的路,也指人所说的话。道可以理解为人与世界打交道的方式。这种方式其实没有办法命名和言说,即人与世界交往的原始状态无法言说。道不是名称,而是人们路途中行走的路,人从一开始行走和说话,道就将他们与世界联系在了一起。无论是古汉语还是拉丁语,行走和说话同的都是同一个词。所以,从这个意义上来讲,道和拉丁语的 logos(意思是理据背后的逻辑)具有相通性。

B4. Culture Highlights

Q: *One of the main ideas of Taoism is the belief in balancing forces, or yin and yang. What is the principle of it?*

A: The principle of Yin and Yang is that all things exist as inseparable and contradictory opposites, for example, female-male, dark-light and old-young. The pairs of equal opposites attract and complement each other. The principle dates from the 3rd century BCE or even earlier and is a fundamental concept in Chinese philosophy, Chinese medicine, and culture in general.

As the Yin and Yang symbol illustrates, each side has at its core an element of the other (represented by the small dots). Neither pole is superior to the other and, as an increase in one brings a corresponding decrease in the other, a correct balance between the two poles must be reached in order to achieve harmony.

The concept of Yin and Yang and the idea of complementary forces became popular with the work of the Chinese school of Yinyang which studied philosophy and cosmology in the 3rd century BCE. The principal proponent of the theory was the cosmologist Zou Yan (or Tsou Yen) who believed that life went through five phases (wuxing) — fire, water, metal, wood, earth — which continuously interchanged according to the principle of Yin and Yang.

(Adapted from *worldhistory.org*)

Q: *Taoism and Confucianism are very similar in many core beliefs. What are the major differences?*

A:Even though Taoism and Confucianism are very similar in many core beliefs, they are different in significant ways. A refusal to participate in strict rites and rituals sets Taoism apart most dramatically from the philosophy of Confucius. Koller writes:

Confucius advocated rites and music so that the desires and emotions might be developed and regulated, for therein lay the development of humanity. To Lao Tzu, efforts to develop and regulate the desires and emotions seemed artificial, tending to interfere with the harmony of nature. Rather than organize and regulate things to achieve perfection, Lao-Tzu advocated letting things work to their perfection naturally. This means supporting all things in their natural state, allowing them to transform spontaneously.

To Lao Tzu (the name is used here as an expression of Taoist thought), the more regulations one demanded, the harder one made one's life and the lives of others. If one relaxed the artificial rules and regulations which were supposed to improve life, only then would one find that life naturally regulates itself and one would fall into pace with the Tao which runs through and regulates and binds and releases all things naturally.

(Adapted from *worldhistory.org*)

Q: *What are the 4 principles of Taoism?*

A:Like most ancient writing on Taoism, it is difficult to discern who wrote the 4 principles of Taoism. Some attribute them to Lao Tzu. Some maintain that Lao Tzu was a functional character. Either way, they are not dissimilar to the Four Stoic Virtues, in that they serve as moral signposts for living life in accordance with nature. Here are the 4 principles of Taoism.

Kindness

Kindness in words creates confidence.

Kindness in thinking creates wisdom.

Kindness in giving creates love.

Essentially, being gentle means giving up the need to be right; being kind is more important than being correct and asserting your own beliefs. When we are gentle, we stop trying to dominate others and instead live in harmony with others. Empty your boat!

Natural Serenity

When pure sincerity (authenticity) forms within, it is outwardly realized in other people's hearts. Without being authentic, we can't live in harmony. Being swayed by outside forces makes us lose sight of who we really are and who we want to be. By accepting the truth about ourselves and others, we not only find peace in this life but we can help others along their paths as well.

Reverence for All Life

Living in the moment brings you a sense of reverence for all of life's blessings. Chuang Tzu believed that respecting all forms of life was essential for harmony: "All creation and creatures are equally important and they require equal respect." Trying to dominate and control all life only leads you away from enlightenment. You can't find peace in the midst of a struggle for control. A truly spiritual perspective tells us that love is freedom.

Supportiveness

Be supportive, but let go of the outcome. Just like the other virtues, supportiveness applies to everything and everyone, including ourselves. It allows us to come from a healthier place and to be there for others who might need help along their own path.

(Adapted from *mindfulstoic.net*)

Q: *Except for Taoism, there are many other influential schools of thought in China. What are they?*

A: Confucianism

Confucianism was founded by Confucius who believed that human beings were essentially good and only strayed due to lack of a strong moral standard. If people were thoroughly instructed in how to develop their own individual moral standard, and the ways in which to adhere to that standard, they would then consistently behave well. Confucianism, therefore, stressed the importance of ritual. One could become "good" by observing rituals which made one "good". One's adherence to these rituals, whether one cared for them or not, built a strong, moral character which would contribute to a strong, moral community and this would contribute to a sound, moral, and stable state, which would result in the highest level of prosperity and happiness for all.

Legalism

Legalism, founded by Han Feizi but based on earlier principles attributed to Yang Mang of the state of Qin, rejects the tenets of both Confucianism and Taoism in maintaining that humans act only out of self-interest and require strict laws in order to control their natural impulses toward engaging in bad behavior. Left on one's own, legalism maintains, one will do whatever one likes, regardless of potential circumstance or whomever else might be harmed. The only defense against the chaos of people pursuing their own self-interest is the law which promised harsh penalties for those who failed to observe it to the letter.

Mohism

Mohism was founded by Mo Ti (also given as Mot Tzu, Mozi, and Micius) and emphasized universal love as the means to better one's self and one's community as well as the concept of consequentialism (one's actions define one's character as the standard of determining of who is "good" and who is "bad"). Mo Ti attempted to neutralize the various Warring States by providing them with the same defenses and strategies so that none would gain an advantage, would recognize the futility of war, and agree to live in peace. He hoped that the rulers of each state would choose universal love, whereby everyone was treated as a member of one's own family.

(Adapted from *worldhistory.org*)

B5. Extension

Extensive Reading

Passage One

Ancient Chinese Philosophy

The term Ancient Chinese Philosophy refers to the belief systems developed by various philosophers during the era known as the Hundred Schools of Thought when these thinkers formed their own schools during the Spring and Autumn Period (772-476 BCE) and the Warring States Period (481-221 BCE) after the Zhou Dynasty (1046-256 BCE) had begun to decline.

The term Hundred Schools of Thought should be understood figuratively to mean "many", not literally. The ten schools which developed from this period were:

- Confucianism
- Taoism

- Legalism
- Mohism
- School of Names
- Yin-Yang School
- School of Minor Talks
- School of Diplomacy
- Agriculturalism
- Syncretism

In addition to these, there were minor schools which attracted adherents but were never formally established:

- Yangism (Hedonist School)
- Relativism
- School of the Military
- School of Medicine

Out of these 14, three would gain prominence and influence— Confucianism, Taoism, and Legalism — and either condemn the others outright or absorb their central concepts in whole or in part. The Warring States Period ended when the state of Qin defeated the other six states and founded the Qin Dynasty (221-206 BCE). Around 213 BCE, the Qin emperor, Shi Huangdi (221-210 BCE) ordered all the books from the Hundred Schools of Thought burned except those on Legalism, his own personal philosophy which became that of the state. The works of the other schools which survived the period known as "The Burning of the Books and Burying of Scholars" only did so because they were hidden by people at great personal risk.

The Qin Dynasty was succeeded by the Han Dynasty (202 BCE-220 CE), which revived learning and an interest in the various philosophical schools of thought. Under the Han emperor Wu Ti (also known as Wu the Great, 141-87 BCE), Confucianism was adopted as the state philosophy and would go on, along with Taoism and Legalism, to inform Chinese culture up through the present day.

Warring States & Schools of Thought

The Zhou Dynasty began as a centralized government under King Wu (1046-1043 BCE) but was greatly expanded by his brother, the Duke of Wu (1042-1035 BCE) who succeeded him. The revolts which erupted following the Duke of Wu's conquests, and the vast territory the Zhou now held, encouraged a change of plan and the Chinese government was decentralized and reorganized as a feudal system in which lords, loyal to the king, governed nearly autonomous states. This worked well as long as the lords were bound by their oaths of loyalty but, in time, the states grew more powerful than the king and the oaths were forgotten as royal authority declined.

The so-called Western Zhou period (1046-771 BCE) transitioned to the Eastern Zhou period (771-256 BCE) when barbarians (probably the Xirong people of the west) invaded and forced the government to move east for better defense. The first part of the Eastern Zhou Period is known as the Spring and Autumn Period after the name of the state chronicles of the time which recorded these events.

The Spring and Autumn Period is the era of the greatest advances in philosophy, Chinese literature, arts, music, and culture overall — even though it was a time of instability — because the scholars and thinkers who were once associated with a state-run organization became displaced, started their own schools (or preached their own vision without a formal school), and attracted followers. As each school of thought differed significantly from the others, this period was later referred to as the time of the Contention of the Hundred Schools of Thought. The term, as scholar Forrest E. Baird notes, suggests "intense philosophical rivalry from the start" as each contended with the others for followers.

(Adapted from *worldhistory.org*)

Passage Two

Zhuangzi: Chinese Daoist Philosopher

Zhuangzi (Chuang-tzu or Master Zhuang), the most significant of China's early interpreters of Daoism, whose work (Zhuangzi) is considered one of the definitive texts of Daoism and is thought to be more comprehensive than the *Tao-Te-Ting*, which is attributed to Laozi, the first philosopher of Daoism. Zhuangzi's teachings also exerted a great influence on the development of Chinese Buddhism and had considerable effect on Chinese landscape painting and poetry.

Life

In spite of his importance, details of Zhuangzi's life, apart from the many anecdotes about him in the Zhuangzi itself, are unknown. The "Grand Historian" of the Han dynasty, Sima Qian incorporated in his biographical sketch of Zhuangzi only the most meagre information. It indicates that Zhuangzi was a native of the state of Meng, that his personal name was Zhou, and that he was a minor official at Qiyuan in his home state. He lived during the reign of Prince Wei of Chu and was therefore a contemporary of Mencius, an eminent Confucian scholar known as China's "Second Sage." According to Sima Qian, Zhuangzi's teachings were drawn primarily from the sayings of Laozi, but his perspective was much broader. He used his literary and philosophical skills to refute the Confucians and Mohists (followers of Mozi, who advocated "concern for everyone").

Zhuangzi is best known through the book that bears his name, *Zhuangzi*, also known as *Nanhua zhenjing*. At about the turn of the 4th century CE, Guo Xiang, the first and perhaps the best commentator on the *Zhuangzi*, established the work as a primary source for Daoist thought. It is composed of 33 chapters, and evidence suggests that there may have been as many as 53 chapters in copies of the book circulated in the 4th century. It is generally agreed that the first seven chapters, the "inner books," are for the most part from the hand of Zhuangzi himself, whereas the "outer books" (chapters 8-22) and the miscellany (chapters 23-33) are largely the product of his later followers. A vivid description of Zhuangzi's character comes from the anecdotes about him in the book's later chapters.

Character

Zhuangzi appears in these passages as an unpredictable and eccentric sage who seems careless about personal comforts or public esteem. His clothing is shoddy and patched, and his shoes have to be tied to his feet with string in order to keep them from falling apart. Nevertheless, he does not consider himself to be miserable, only poor. When his good friend Hui Shi comes to console him upon the death of his wife, he finds the sage sitting on a mat, singing and beating on a basin. Hui Shi reprimands him, pointing out that such behavior is improper at the death of someone who has lived and grown old with him and has borne him children.

When Zhuangzi himself was at the point of death, his disciples began to talk about an elaborate burial for him. Zhuangzi immediately stopped the discussion by declaring that he did not need the paraphernalia of a great funeral, that nature would be his inner and outer coffin, the sun and the moon his jade rings, and the stars and the planets his jewelry. All creation would make offerings and escort him. He needed no more. Somewhat taken aback, his disciples declared that they were afraid that the crows and the buzzards might eat him. To this Zhuangzi replied, "Above the ground it's the crows and the kites who will eat me; below the ground it's the worms and the ants. What prejudice is this, that you wish to take from the one to give to the other?"

Zhuangzi's eccentricities stem directly from his understanding of the processional nature of human experience. Insight for Zhuangzi comes with the realization that everything in life is both dynamic and continuous — what he calls dao.

Philosophy

Zhuangzi taught that what can be known or said of the Dao is not the Dao. It has neither initial beginning nor final end, nor limitations or demarcations. Life is the ongoing transformation of the Dao, in which there is no better or worse, no good or evil. Things should be allowed to follow their own course, and men should not value one situation over another. A truly virtuous man is free from the bondage of circumstance, personal attachments, tradition, and the need to reform his world. Zhuangzi declined an offer to be prime minister of the state of Chu because he did not want the entanglements of a court career.

The relativity of all experience is in constant tension in the Zhuangzi with the unity of all things. When asked where the Dao was, Zhuangzi replied that it was everywhere. When pushed to be more specific, he declared that it was in ants and, still lower, in weeds and potsherds; furthermore, it was also in excrement and urine. This forceful statement of the omnipresence of the Dao had its parallels in later Chinese Buddhism, in which a similar figure of speech was used to describe the ever-present Buddha (Buddhist scholars, especially those of the Chan [Zen] school, also drew heavily on Zhuangzi's works). Zhuangzi was par excellence the philosopher of the unattached man who is at one with the Dao.

(Adapted from *britannica.com*)

B6. Assignment

Brochure Design

Form groups of 3 or 4 and **design an English brochure on Daoism.** The major parts might include:

- A brief introduction of Daoism
- Key figures of Daoism
- The influence of Daoism

References

Berling, J. A. (2022). Confucianism. Retrieved from https://asiasociety.org/education/confucianism on February 23rd, 2022.

Berling, J. A. (2022). Daoism. The way. Retrieved from https://asiasociety.org/education/daoism on February 23rd, 2022.

CGTN (2021). China's "Double Reduction" Policy: Impacts of the New Regulations for Off-Campus Tutoring in Core School Subjects. Retrieved from https://news.cgtn.com/news/2021-08-22/VHJhbnNjcmlwdDU3ODM1/index.html on March 4th, 2022.

Cartwright, M. (2012). Confucius. Retrieved from https://www.worldhistory.org/Confucius/ on March 4th, 2022.

Cohen, M. (1976). Confucius and Socrates. *Journal of Chinese Philosophy*. D. Reidel Publishing Company, Dordrecht-Holland.

Confucian Thought on Heaven and Humanity (2022). Retrieved from https://simulation.toys/zh/confucian-thought-on-heaven-and-humanity.html on March 4th, 2022.

Editors of Encyclopedia Britannica (2022). Tian, Chinese Religion. Retrieved from https://www.britannica.com/topic/tian on March 1st, 2022.

Jen & Li (2022). Jen & Li-Confucian Virtues. Retrieved from https://www.world-religions-professor.com/jen.html on March 6th, 2022.

Mack, L. (2019). Filial Piety: An important Chinese Cultural Value. Retrieved from https://www.thoughtco.com/filial-piety-in-chinese-688386 on March 1st, 2022.

MacRae, C. (2021). Who was Chuang Tzu? Badass Philosopher, but not a Taoist. Retrieved from https://mindfulstoic.net/who-was-chuang-tzu/ on March 4th, 2022.

Mark, E. (2016). Taoism. Retrieved from https://www.worldhistory.org/Taoism/ on March 4th, 2022.

Standford Encyclopedia of Philosophy (2020). Confucius. Retrieved from https://plato.stanford.edu/entries/confucius/ on March 4th, 2022.

Study.com (2022). Confucianism Beliefs, Symbols & Facts. Retrieved from https://study.com/academy/lesson/confucianism-definition-beliefs-history.html on March 1st, 2022.

Tan, C. (2017). Confucianism and Education. Retrieved from https://oxfordre.com/education/view/10.1093/acrefore/9780190264093.001.0001/acrefore-9780190264093-e-226? print on March 4th, 2022.

The Economist (2021). China Urges Its People to Struggle. Some Say No. Retrieved from https://www.economist.com/china/2021/07/03/china-urges-its-people-to-struggle-some-say-no on March 4th, 2022.

Ware, J.H. (2022). Zhuangzi, Chinese Daoist Philosopher. Retrieved from https://www.britannica.com/biography/Zhuangzi on March 5th, 2022.

Wuwei (2019). Wu Wei: The Art of Non-action. Retrieved from https://exploringyourmind.com/wu-wei-the-art-of-non-action/ on March 4th, 2022.